Tyra
Banks

Other books in the People in the News series:

Tyra Banks

by Terri Dougherty

LUCENT BOOKS
A part of Gale, Cengage Learning

GALE
CENGAGE Learning™

Detroit • New York • San Francisco • New Haven, Conn • Waterville, Maine • London

© 2010 Gale, Cengage Learning

LIBRARY OF CONGRESS CATALOGING-IN-PUBLICATION DATA

Dougherty, Terri.
  Tyra Banks / by Terri Dougherty.
    p. cm. — (People in the news)
  Includes bibliographical references and index.
  ISBN 978-1-4205-0161-2 (hardcover)
1. Banks, Tyra—Juvenile literature. 2. Models (Persons)—United
States—Biography—Juvenile literature. 3. African American television
personalities—United States—Biography—Juvenile literature. 4. Television
personalities—United States—Biography—Juvenile literature. I. Title.
  HD6073.M77B3642 2009
  746.9'2092—dc22
  [B]
                                                          2009019991

Lucent Books
27500 Drake Rd
Farmington Hills MI 48331

ISBN-13: 978-1-4205-0161-2
ISBN-10: 1-4205-0161-5

Printed in the United States of America
1 2 3 4 5 6 7 13 12 11 10 09

Printed by Bang Printing, Brainerd, MN, 1ˢᵗ Ptg., 11/2009

Contents

Fame and celebrity are alluring. People are drawn to those who walk in fame's spotlight, whether they are known for great accomplishments or for notorious deeds. The lives of the famous pique public interest and attract attention, perhaps because their experiences seem in some ways so different from, yet in other ways so similar to, our own.

Newspapers, magazines, and television regularly capitalize on this fascination with celebrity by running profiles of famous people. For example, television programs such as *Entertainment Tonight* devote all their programming to stories about entertainment and entertainers. Magazines such as *People* fill their pages with stories of the private lives of famous people. Even newspapers, newsmagazines, and television news frequently delve into the lives of well-known personalities. Despite the number of articles and programs, few provide more than a superficial glimpse at their subjects.

Lucent's People in the News series offers young readers a deeper look into the lives of today's newsmakers, the influences that have shaped them, and the impact they have had in their fields of endeavor and on other people's lives. The subjects of the series hail from many disciplines and walks of life. They include authors, musicians, athletes, political leaders, entertainers, entrepreneurs, and others who have made a mark on modern life and who, in many cases, will continue to do so for years to come.

These biographies are more than factual chronicles. Each book emphasizes the contributions, accomplishments, or deeds that have brought fame or notoriety to the individual and shows how that person has influenced modern life. Authors portray their subjects in a realistic, unsentimental light. For example, Bill Gates – the cofounder and chief executive officer of the software giant Microsoft – has been instrumental in making personal computers the most vital tool of the modern age. Few dispute his business savvy, his perseverance, or his technical expertise, yet critics say he is ruthless in his dealings with competitors and driven more by his desire to maintain Microsoft's dominance in the computer industry than by an interest in furthering technology.

In these books, young readers will encounter inspiring stories about real people who achieved success despite enormous obstacles. Oprah Winfrey – the most powerful, most watched, and wealthiest woman on television today – spent the first six years of her life in the care of her grandparents while her unwed mother sought work and a better life elsewhere. Her adolescence was colored by promiscuity, pregnancy at age fourteen, rape, and sexual abuse.

Each author documents and supports his or her work with an array of primary and secondary source quotations taken from diaries, letters, speeches, and interviews. All quotes are footnoted to show readers exactly how and where biographers derive their information and provide guidance for further research. The quotations enliven the text by giving readers eyewitness views of the life and accomplishments of each person covered in the People in the News series.

In addition, each book in the series includes photographs, annotated bibliographies, timelines, and comprehensive indexes. For both the casual reader and the student researcher, the People in the News series offers insight into the lives of today's newsmakers – people who shape the way we live, work, and play in the modern age.

Success to "Bank On"

Tyra Banks has used her career as a supermodel to build a media empire that has her working like a superwoman. The former *Sports Illustrated* swimsuit cover model became a powerful and prominent figure who created a popular talk show in 2005 as she built on the success of her reality television program *America's Next Top Model,* launched in 2003. She has her own television program production company, Banksable Productions, and routinely makes Forbes' list of top-earning celebrities. In 2009 she brought in $30 million and was named one of Forbes' most influential women in media. She does not use her influence randomly, however, but uses it to encourage her values of positive body image and the importance of inner beauty.

From Savvy Model to Glamorous Producer

Banks became known for her sultry good looks and ability to project a powerful and captivating image on the runway and in magazine photos. Her five-foot-ten height and beautiful features contributed to her success, but she also knew how to use her personality to set herself apart from other gorgeous models. She could go from a sexy look to a thoughtful one in a split second and knew more than a hundred ways to deliver a smile. She was also wise enough to realize that her modeling career would not last forever.

Even while modeling in Paris, Tyra was thinking about her long-term career.

Almost from the time she arrived in Paris to look for modeling work at age seventeen, Banks has taken a long-term approach to her career. She began working the runway for big names in fashion, such as designers Yves Saint Laurent, Oscar de la Renta, and Chanel, but did not stop there. She knew that this was only the first step in her career, and, when her curves hindered her ability to work in high fashion, she found even more success in commercial work. She struck a deal with Cover Girl and also became the first black model to grace the covers of *Sports Illustrated, GQ,* and the Victoria's Secret catalog.

Banks was successful as a model, but was also interested in where her reputation could take her. An interest in television had been with her since high school, and she dabbled in acting. Her career leaped to new levels when she moved behind the camera to produce shows of her own. She developed—and stars in—two popular programs, *America's Next Top Model* and *The Tyra Banks Show.*

When Banks began producing television shows, she did not simply provide the financial backing for projects to see her name on them. She was passionate about her ideas and became involved in the programs' details, even loaning her own clothing to the *America's Next Top Model* contestants. She continues to be fierce and demanding as she schools the models, urging them to do their best and adding to the drama that attracts viewers.

The Girl Next Door

On her talk show, Banks goes against the aloof supermodel stereotype to become a girlfriend next door who loves to share advice and divulge secrets. She reveals the goofy and outgoing sides of her personality and is not afraid admit she has flaws and imperfections. She also shows viewers the vulnerable side of her personality, and she teared up when she reacted to comments others had made about her weight. In addition, Banks is not afraid to do things that surprise her audience. She showed how her photos were retouched to take away cellulite and went out in public in a fat suit to make a point about body image.

Banks has indicated that she wants to do more than produce shows; she also has a message to deliver. Aware that the lean body image models project could hurt girls' self-esteem, she saw that she had the power to confront body image stereotypes and help young girls and women feel confident about their looks. Through a "So What?" campaign on her talk show and her TZONE Foundation, she developed programs that make girls and women proud of who they are and what they look like.

Banks also promotes the theme of inner beauty on shows she produces but does not star in. Reality programs such as *True Beauty* and *Stylista* project the theme that there is more to beauty than good looks. These shows about the world of beauty contests and of fashion magazines have a glamorous edge to them. However, they also stress the importance of solid moral values and inner qualities that contribute to making a person's image a beautiful one. On *True Beauty* contestants who thought they were being judged only by how they looked were actually being judged on both their appearance and how they treated others. On *Sylista* those hoping for an internship at fashion magazine *Elle* had to prove they were worthy of the job.

The Tyra Banks Show *was geared to promote self confidence.*

Since her beginnings as a runway star, Banks has become a hard-working, clever media mogul with a conscience. Confident about her body, she wants to help other women be confident about theirs. She's the big sister that girls and women can confide in and turn to for advice, and she has turned her passion for delivering guidance into a media empire. Beginning with *America's Next Top Model* and extending to her talk show and other reality programs she produces, she shares what she has learned and tries to make women feel better about themselves. She spices up her message of self-respect with a helping of glamour to create intriguing programs and, in doing so, has become one of the entertainment industry's most powerful and influential women.

Gangly Girl, Beautiful Model

Tyra Lynne Banks came into this world a California girl. Born on December 4, 1973, she grew up in Inglewood, California, a suburb of Los Angeles. Her hometown is southwest of Los Angeles, near Long Beach Harbor, and is home to about 130,000 people.

Tyra grew up in a middle class family. Her mother, Carolyn, worked as a medical photographer at a jet propulsion lab for NASA and her father, Don, was a computer consultant. Tyra also has a brother, Devin, who is seven years older than she is.

Tyra was very close with her mother growing up.

Tyra's parents divorced when she was six, and, although she lived with her mother, Tyra's father remained part of her life. She lived with her mother during the week and her father on weekends. She felt loved by both parents. She sometimes wished they would get back together, but she also realized that they were happier and less tense when they were apart.

Her mother eventually remarried, and Cliff London became Tyra's stepfather. He was strict with Tyra and made sure she did chores such as keeping her room clean and washing the dishes before bed. She resented his authority at first, but eventually learned to get along with him and appreciate the discipline.

Fourth-Grade Bully

Tyra got along well with her parents, but her brother was a source of frustration for her when she was young. They did not have a very friendly relationship because her brother bullied her and bossed her around. He ate the meat and potatoes off her plate, leaving her with only vegetables, or teased her about being clumsy.

When Tyra's brother picked on her, she felt powerless because he was so much older than she was. He stood up for his sister, however, and she came to see that he was a good person to have on her side. "No matter how much Devin taunts and teases me, I always know he's got my back," she said. "He has defended me to the end when anyone has tried to hurt me."[1]

Tyra's rivalry with her brother affected the way she treated her friends at school, however. By fourth grade she had become a bully looking to be in charge. To make sure she remained in control, Tyra put down anyone who got in her way. She was the leader of a pack of about ten girls who listened to what she said and followed her lead. "I was popular, gossipy—and if I didn't want one of the other girls to be in the clique anymore, for whatever tiny little reason, I voted her out," Banks admitted.[2] Tyra's attempt to be in control and gain power sometimes had other girls in tears.

Tyra the Critic

As a young girl, Tyra Banks was already thinking about how she could make the world a better place. She had ideas for improving everything from television commercials to her classmates' bathing habits. She did not always deliver her advice in a constructive way, however.

In fourth grade Tyra took a seat in class that had belonged to a girl who had a body odor problem and yelled, "She stinks, she stinks!" She got in trouble with both her teacher and her mother and got into even bigger trouble the next day when she tried to make the situation better. She told the girl about proper hygiene, but the principal did not like her approach. "She said, 'How dare you tell somebody how to clean herself!'" Tyra recalled. "I'm sure I told the girl in a mean way because I remember that she cried."

Tyra Banks, "Confessions of a Former Mean Girl," *Teen People*, October 2005, p. 52.

Learning Her Lesson

When she was young Tyra was a leader among her friends at school, but it was not long before she learned what it felt like to be picked on by her peers. When she was eleven, her father lost his job, so she had to leave a small private school and attend a public school with 2,000 students. Tyra was faced with making new friends and trying to figure out how she fit in.

A growth spurt complicated Tyra's move to the new school. She grew several inches over the summer months and became tall and slender. She was so tall and skinny by the end of the summer that her old friends did not even recognize her. "I went from being the popular girl who looked normal to being considered a freak," Tyra recalled. "I was gawky and skinny, and the kids stared at me and were like, 'What's wrong with you?'"[3]

Tyra was often ridiculed for her looks in school, growing taller and being thinner than those around her.

Tyra continued to grow as she entered middle school. She sprouted to five-foot-nine and weighed ninety-eight pounds. Other kids taunted her with the nickname "Ethiopia" because she looked like a person enduring the Ethiopian famine. She was also called "Olive Oil" because of her stature and "Fivehead" because her forehead was so large. Others thought she had an eating disorder because she looked so thin.

Tyra's looks made her feel unsure of herself, and she found it difficult to fit in. She did not want to leave the house and sometimes just wanted to stay in her bedroom because her looks attracted stares. At school she would not change into gym clothes because she did not want other girls to see her body. At home even an offhand comment from her mother about her skinniness caused her to shut herself away in her bedroom.

The former popular girl and bully was learning what it was like to be on the other side of things. Rather than picking on other girls, she was dealing with insecurity and being called names herself. She felt rejected and alone.

Tyra later reflected that the shift in her popularity did have a positive side, as it caused her to become a kinder person. Because she was no longer popular and now knew what it was like to be picked on, she changed her attitude toward others. "Experiencing the pain of being picked on turned me around," she said. "It turned out that the best things in my life were to be made fun of, and to have no friends, and to feel miserable every single day. It made me compassionate."[4]

Model Ideas

Tyra's social life improved as she got older and became kinder, and things turned around for her in high school. Although she was still tall and thin, her body filled out. At five-foot-ten and 110 pounds, she was still uncertain about her looks, but she gained more friends.

Tyra eventually returned to private school. She attended Immaculate Heart High School, a Catholic girls' school in Los Angeles. On the first day of class, a girl who was impressed by her looks asked Tyra if she had ever considered modeling. At first Tyra thought it was a crazy idea, but, as she thought about it more seriously, she decided it to give it a try.

Tyra's mother supported the idea. Because Carolyn London was a photographer, it was not difficult for the mother and daughter to put together a portfolio of photos of Tyra that they could take to modeling agencies. After London took the pictures of Tyra looking like a model, she and Tyra put them into a portfolio and began knocking on doors.

When they showed Tyra's photographs to modeling agencies, Tyra and her mother were initially met with a cool reception. The agents commented that Tyra was not photogenic enough to become a model. They insisted that they already had enough black models. "I'd leave these places crying," Tyra said. "But my mom said, 'Look, if it's really something you want to do, use the rejection as motivation.'"[5]

Tyra did not let the negative comments from the agents derail her plan to model. She saw modeling as a skill she could improve on and worked at delivering the right look and smile in her photos.

Model in the Making

After Carolyn London was done working for the day, Tyra's photographer mother sometimes took pictures of her children. When Tyra looked at the photos after she was older, she could see hints of a model-to-be in the pictures. "When I look at those pictures, I realize I am posing," she says. "I have my hand on my chin and I'm looking right at the camera."

Tyra's mom also had a small photography business at home and took portraits in her living room. Tyra helped out by holding the light meters and reflectors and watched as her mother developed the film in a darkroom on their back porch. "It's so funny that the little assistant holding the lights was a supermodel in the making," Tyra says.

Tyra Banks and Vanessa Thomas Bush, "What Matters Most in My Work and My Life," *Newsweek*, October 20, 2008, p. 54.

She and her mother continued visiting agents and showing them her portfolio. By the time she was in eleventh grade, she had met with success. Banks signed with a modeling agency and got her first job for the magazine *Black Collegiate*. "I was so excited because there was a little picture of me on the cover, above the title," Banks says.[6]

Career Options

Tyra kept modeling in high school, working for fashion catalogs and young adult magazines such as *Seventeen*. Although her after-school job was in a glamorous profession, Tyra did not let her modeling keep her from paying attention to her schoolwork, and the classes she took at Immaculate Heart prepared her for college.

When Tyra thought about careers, one that interested her was working in television or film. When she had been younger, she had been intrigued by television commercials and the way they were written, and, when she was in high school, a career as a producer or writer in the entertainment industry intrigued her. When she was modeling, she also thought it would be nice to be behind the camera and have control. Although she enjoyed modeling, when she considered life after high school, she knew she did not think she could rely on modeling as a steady job. She was interested in the entertainment industry and leaned toward moving in that direction. "I applied to college because I wanted to be a film/television producer and writer," she said.[7]

During her senior year of high school, Tyra applied to five colleges and was accepted at all of them. When it came time to decide where to continue her education, she chose Loyola Marymount University. The private Catholic university is located on the west side of Los Angeles and has been ranked as one of the best schools in the country.

Breakthrough

Although Tyra had been accepted at a top college, she kept working as a model. She had been signed by the L.A. Models Agency, and, shortly before she was due to begin her college classes, a visitor to the agency changed those plans.

Tyra left for Paris instead of attending college, confident that she had "the look" of a model.

Two weeks before school started at Loyola, a model scout from France visited the modeling agency in Los Angeles that represented Tyra. He saw her photo and encouraged her to find work at the haute couture shows in Paris. Tyra recalled that he was very decisive about his choice. "[He] came to the modeling agency in L.A., saw my picture and said, 'That's the only girl I want,'" Tyra said.[8]

Tyra now had a decision to make. She could stay in the United States, attend college, and work toward a career in television, or she could take a chance and look for work as a model in Paris. Lured by the adventure of travel and international modeling, she decided to set her college plans aside. She signed with the Elite modeling agency, the largest agency in the world, and headed to Paris. The seventeen-year-old saw the opportunity as not only a chance to make a career in modeling but as a chance to see the world. Even if she did not find work, she would still have the opportunity to experience Paris. Tyra also agreed to take this chance because she thought she had the right look. "Models are tall, they have a big forehead, their chin is small, they have full lips," she said. "I knew I had that look."[9]

No Modeling School for Tyra

With input from her photographer mother, Tyra Banks taught herself to model. She worked on her runway walk at home and watched videos to get the right posture and poses. She did not attend modeling school and was blunt about the reason why when she was interviewed years later. "I don't believe in them," she said. "Usually, they just take your money." Instead of modeling school, she had other advice for teens considering modeling as a career. "Before pursuing any career, you should graduate from high school," she said.

Renee Minus White, "Tyra Tips off Teens with New Beauty Book," *New Amdsterdam News*, April 9, 1998, p. 17.

Getting Ready

Tyra did some homework before heading to Paris. She knew that the city represented a huge opportunity for her and that modeling was more than putting on beautiful clothes and walking down a runway. Before she left, her mother encouraged her to learn more about how runway models looked, acted, and worked. To prepare for Paris, Tyra got videos from a fashion design school and watched how the models posed and walked. She also studied pictures in French fashion magazines and at her mother's urging learned the names of people who worked in the business, such as the hairdressers, makeup artists, and photographers who had their names in fashion magazines. She studied the top designers and also watched the style shows on MTV to get tips on how to look and act when she was on the runway.

To achieve a strut that would interest the designers, Tyra paraded across the living room while wearing her mother's high heels and long nightgowns. Her mother's coaching helped her develop a style that reflected her personality. Tyra admitted that she did not look like a supermodel during those early practice sessions. "My ankles would shake and I would bend my knees and stick my lips out," she said.[10]

Although a model scout had suggested Tyra go to Paris to look for work, she knew that there was no guarantee any of the fashion shows would hire her. She prepared as best she could but realized it could take time to break into the business. Tyra gave herself a year to find work as a model. If she did not get work by then, she planned to return home and go to college.

Tyra had come a long way from the skinny girl who did not want to leave her bedroom. She was no longer the mean girl who had picked on others or the insecure teen who had felt like a geek. She now had enough confidence in her looks and herself to head to a different country to try to establish a career. She might encounter rejection, but she could also have the opportunity to work with some of the world's top clothing designers.

Chapter 2

High-Fashion Model

Banks left for Paris in September 1991. The seventeen-year-old headed for Europe on her own, without a chaperone, to start a new chapter in her life. The once insecure schoolgirl was now traveling to Europe as an aspiring model hoping to hit the runway.

Once she arrived in Paris, Banks did not waste any time looking for work. She had prepared by studying the designers and other aspects of the business of fashion. She was now ready to put her knowledge to work. She knew the names of the people in the industry, and whom she wanted to get in touch with. She was not in the city to vacation but to find employment. As she applied and interviewed for work in fashion shows and met other models in the industry, she found both success and painful surprises.

Fresh Face

Banks went on a number of "go-sees" after arriving in Paris. At these appointments set up by her agency, she interviewed for the chance to be a runway model in a fashion show. Banks soon realized that she was not like the other girls who were trying out for the Paris fashion shows. Her different looks and down-to-earth attitude set her apart from other models.

She had a more easygoing mood than many of the other modeling hopefuls. She went to interviews without makeup

*While in Paris, Tyra admitted other models were more
beautiful than her, but she thought she had a more
unique look.*

and dressed casually in overalls, hiking boots, and plaid shirts, whereas other aspiring models showed up in high heels and fashionable clothes. She found it more practical and comfortable to dress casually. "I couldn't understand how they could run around the city from appointment to appointment all day long, usually on the subway, in confining clothes and heels," she said.[11]

The five-foot-ten Banks also looked different from many of the other models. She had ebony skin and a large forehead.

On Her Own

While she was living in Paris, Banks did a good job of keeping herself focused on her work, but not everything was going smoothly. She found modeling to be a lonely business, as she was often alone when she visited fashion designers and prepared for shows.

She did not make many friends among the other models who were also looking for work in the high fashion industry. "Actresses or singers travel with entourages, with their hair and makeup people and tour managers. Models are alone," Banks said. "Even when you're the biggest supermodel in the world, you're alone. I tried to get to L.A. and hang out with my high-school friends as often as I could."

On her own for the first time, she also struggled with making meals and did a poor job of eating the right things. She did not know how to shop for food or prepare her own meals, so she ate the cookies and snacks her mother sent in care packages.

When her mother came for a visit, things got better, because Carolyn London taught her daughter how to cook. Thanks to her mother's intervention, Banks's cookie diet changed to something more nutritious.

Tyra Banks and Vanessa Thomas Bush, "What Matters Most in My Work and My Life," *Newsweek*, October 20, 2008, p. 54.

She admitted that there were other girls at the go-sees who were more beautiful. These differences, however, worked in her favor, because Banks offered the designers a refreshing change. When designers looked at her, they saw something they liked. "When I started modeling, I definitely wasn't the prettiest girl in the room," she said. "I was tall, skinny, and had a huge fore-head—a little odd looking. But the fashion industry embraced me because I wasn't so typical."[12]

Winning Personality

The fashion designers Banks visited liked her personality and the fact that it came through when she walked the runway. Banks knew how to bring something different to her runway walk, and her stage presence was met with approval from highly respect-ed fashion designers. She could catch people's attention, and at the same time was graceful and stylish. "She reminds me of an antelope," designer Todd Oldham said. "She was just born with grace."[13]

Banks's interesting look and graceful, confident runway walk brought her success. Fashion designers were eager to have the young model in their shows. Within a few weeks of arriving in Paris, Banks was booked for two dozen runway shows as well as photo shoots for magazine covers. In her first season as a model, Banks worked for some of the largest names in the fashion industry. She modeled clothing for iconic fashion houses such as Karl Lagerfeld, Yves Saint Laurent, Oscar de la Renta, and Chanel. In addition, she appeared on the covers of the European versions of *Cosmopolitan* and *Elle*.

The strong impression Banks had made during the go-sees carried over to the shows. When Banks was on the runway, people noticed. She brought both personality and beauty to the catwalk and quickly earned the respect of those in the fashion and advertising industries. "Tyra knows her role on the runway: She entertains but at the same time she knows that she's there to sell. And she does just that," said former runway model Bethann Hardison.[14]

Tyra Banks conveyed her confidence and beauty on the runways of Paris.

Model Business

Banks's runway presence helped her get work in Paris, but that was not the only reason she found success there. She was only seventeen, but she put work before pleasure. When she had a show to prepare for, she concentrated on getting ready for it.

The fascinating sights and entertainment of Paris did not distract her. When she was booked for fashion shows, she resisted the temptation to enjoy the city's night life. She did not go out to nightclubs and, if she wanted to go out, she went to a movie, hoping to find one in English. By 10 P.M. she would be in bed. Banks was aware that modeling is a business and, if she was going to be successful, she needed to concentrate on her work.

The Jealous Competition

Banks did what it took to find work as a model, and her efforts were met with success, but not everyone was happy about her sudden popularity on the runway. Although she was consistently a favorite of fashion designers, she had to endure some negative comments from other models who were also looking to book shows and work with the top designers. As more fashion designers asked for Banks to be in their shows and her work on the runway attracted attention, other models feared that she would take the spotlight away from them. Even more established high-fashion models felt threatened by the newcomer.

Some models resorted to using tricks to keep Banks off the runway, such as not telling her when a photo shoot started. Banks considered these actions to be petty and resolved to stay away from this negative behavior herself. "I felt the negative attitudes of other models—older models who didn't like me and didn't really want me to succeed," she said. "I vowed that I wouldn't do that to another girl."[15]

One model who did not treat Banks kindly was Naomi Campbell. Campbell, who was three years older than Banks and had been modeling since she was fifteen, was the reigning black supermodel when Banks came on the scene. She asked that Banks not work in the same shows she did and also wanted Banks to leave the Elite modeling agency so they would not be represented by the same firm.

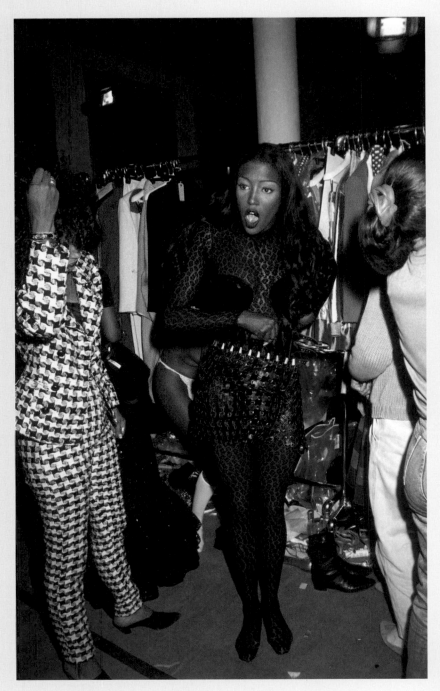

Supermodel Naomi Campbell would not work the same shows as Banks.

A Friendly Face

Banks learned that modeling was hard work and that it could be an emotionally painful business, but her strong work ethic and runway presence helped her continue to find work in fashion shows. While some models were resentful of her success, she maintained an approachable nature that eventually helped her make some friends on the runway.

Model Heidi Klum was one model who said she found Banks to be friendly. Klum and Banks modeled together when they were Victoria's Secret models, and Klum appreciated the fact that she could come to Banks with questions about the business side of the industry. If Klum wondered whom to use for an accountant, attorney, or business manager, she turned to Banks. "Not everyone was, let's say, superfriendly, but Tyra was always nice. She shared her experience and knowledge with me. In this industry there are a lot of people who don't want to help each other, but I guess Tyra was and is secure because she was always willing to share what she had learned," Klum said.

Heidi Klum, "Supermogul with A Business Model," *Time,* May 8, 2006, p. 158.

Banks was upset and frustrated by the situation. She did not lay all the blame on Campbell's shoulders however. She also blamed it on designers who saw both Banks and Campbell simply as interchangeable black models rather than individuals who offered different styles. "No model should have to endure what I went through at 17," Banks said. "It's very sad that the fashion business and press can't accept that there can be more than one reigning black supermodel at a time. People compared us everywhere I went, so there was constant tension between us."[16]

Concerns about Racism

The comparisons to Campbell were not the only times Banks was seen as a black model rather than an individual. Designers wanted her to be in their runway shows, but although she was a sought-after model she did not always make as much money on the runway as the top white models did. In addition, when she looked beyond the runway for work, she found that American magazines were not eager to have a black woman on the cover. She commented that she could get more magazine work in Europe than America and hoped that the United States would come to appreciate the beauty of her ethnic looks.

Banks did not let these difficulties hold her back, however. She did not want to abandon her growing career because of racism or jealousy in the modeling industry. Instead, she focused on her work and persevered to help black models who would follow her into the business. "I've detached myself from the nonsense that goes along with being a black model in this business," Banks says. "I think things will change for the black models who come after us. They won't have to feel so insecure about losing their spots. They'll benefit from our pain."[17]

Calling on Mom

One person who helped Banks deal with the difficulties of the modeling industry was her mother, Carolyn London. When Tyra Banks started modeling, she was hurt and confused by the drama that went on behind the scenes in the world of modeling and unprepared for the backlash that she met when she had success. She dealt with these uncertainties by turning to her mother.

When Banks was new to working in Paris, she phoned her mother and confided in her about the problems she was going through with the other models in the industry. As the situation worsened, she did not want to go through this alone. She asked her mother to move to Paris.

Carolyn London left her position as a medical photographer and came to Europe to become her daughter's business manger. Tyra Banks had to deal with issues such as Campbell's request that she leave the Elite agency, so Carolyn helped her find a new agency to work with. Tyra signed with IMB Models. Later, she

Banks called on her mom to help manage her Paris modeling career.

and her mother founded the Tygirl company to help her manage the demands on her time.

Changing Looks and a New Focus

As Banks's career progressed, there were more things for her and her mother to manage. She worked as a runway model for several years and also appeared on magazine covers. As Banks entered her twenties, however, she found it difficult to maintain the long, lean body that high-fashion designers were after. Her body had begun to change. She became curvier, and some designers shied away from booking her because of the width of her hips. She overheard two seamstresses at one show in Milan calling her fat, even though she weighed only 126 pounds.

Banks tried to regain the slender look that had helped her get modeling jobs when she had first arrived in Paris only three years before. She attempted to keep her weight down by dieting and eating low-calorie foods such as salad with chicken, but her appetite won when she became too hungry to stick to a strict diet. "I was going against my natural habits, and the food didn't satisfy me," she said. "It didn't feel right."[18]

Banks's efforts to lose weight were not enough for the fashion designers she had worked for. Several refused to work with her, and the modeling agency she was working with asked her to lose an additional ten pounds. Banks, who was twenty-two at the time, felt her weight was healthy, but could not deny that it was interfering with her ability to get work on the runway. She and her mother discussed the situation over a meal of pizza in Milan, Italy. Her mother was reluctant to have her daughter slim down. "I [had] sat backstage during the fashion shows, and I would watch young girls with hip bones that protruded so far it made me wonder if it was painful," her mother said. "Before I let her go that route, I said, 'Let's work with what you've got.'"[19]

Rather than conform to her modeling agency's request that she slim down, Banks took her career in a new direction. She and her mother looked for other options for the experienced model. By now Banks had worked in high fashion for several years and knew the ins and outs of the industry. She was familiar with the business side of fashion and the drama that went along with being a model. She had become admired for the personality she brought to the runway and knew that asset would help in future prospects.

Banks soon showed that she was a savvy businesswoman as well as an attractive model. The runways of Paris had given her a start to her career, but now it was time to move on. Rather than try to fit into the world of high fashion, Banks and her mother looked for ways for Tyra to take her career in new directions.

Chapter 3

Supermodel Success

Walking on the runway in the world of high fashion was only one way for Banks to find work as a model. When it became difficult to fit the mold of a runway model, she looked for modeling work where her curvy figure was an asset. She found it through magazines and commercials. Work in advertisements and as a magazine cover model gave her broad media exposure and a nice paycheck. It was not a step down from her work in high fashion but rather a step over to new career opportunities.

Banks believed her experience as a model could also open the door for her in other areas. At one time she had planned to go to college to study television and film and work behind the camera. Now she saw how her work in front of the camera as a model could lead to another job it the entertainment industry: acting. In addition to looking for jobs as a commercial model, she also pursued work in television.

The Right Time for *The Fresh Prince*

Banks was not unfamiliar with the world of television and movies. Soon after she began modeling, her looks, personality, and status as a model had already helped her nab small roles. In 1991 she had a small part in Michael Jackson's video *Black and White*, and she appeared as herself as one of the supermodels in the 1992 British television movie *Inferno*.

Banks, center, played Will Smith's love interest on **The Fresh Prince of Bel-Air.**

Banks said she also had other opportunities to act, but turned the roles down until she found one that was right for her. She found it in 1993, when as a nineteen-year-old, she accepted a recurring role on the sitcom *The Fresh Prince of Bel-Air.* "I wanted to be an actress, director and producer long before I became a model," she said. "By the time I got the role on The Fresh Prince, I had already turned down lots of other parts."[20]

The Fresh Prince starred actor and rapper Will Smith as a teen from Philadelphia who moves to Bel-Air to live with his wealthy relatives after his mother decides he should learn some old-fashioned values from them. Banks played Jackie Ames, the love interest of Will Smith's character. Banks did not have a starring role in the series, but the popular program gave her the opportunity to further her career by gaining experience in television and nationwide exposure in a new medium.

Off-runway Success

Television was not the only way Banks was becoming a familiar face across America at this point in her career. She also found work as a commercial model and appeared on the covers of Elle and Essence magazines. She was in a Ralph Lauren advertisement and in the 1993 swimsuit edition of Sports Illustrated. The next year the twenty-year-old took a significant step with her career by signing a contract with makeup giant Cover Girl.

The Cover Girl contract indicated that Banks was a top-tier model who had the charisma and style needed to be the company's national symbol. When she signed the contract with Cover Girl, Banks became only the second black woman to be a spokesperson for the makeup giant. The move came with a lucrative paycheck and expanded Tyra's visibility, because it put her face in magazine ads and on television commercials all over the United States.

Time for Romance

Banks had a high profile career as a model and actress, and in 1993 began a high-profile relationship as well. When she was nineteen, Banks met movie director John Singleton through mutual friends. Singleton had directed the successful 1991 movie Boyz in the Hood and at age twenty-four had received an Academy

Award nomination for best director. He was a rising star in the film industry, and after he met Banks an initial friendship turned to romance.

Singleton said that he enjoyed being with Banks, because he knew she liked him for who he was, not because of his work as a movie director. Her intelligencee also impressed him. "She has a lot going for her," he said. "I want a woman who's got a mind. Tyra helps me out a lot. She helps me unwind [and eliminate] the stress. It's a real crazy business and it's really good to have somebody who understands how difficult it is."[21] In addition, Banks helped Singleton look at life less seriously. "I tend to be very intense, but she brought out the lighter side in me," Singleton said. "She made me laugh."[22]

Banks's work as a model and his as a director made it difficult for them to be together a great deal of time, but Singleton said they made things work by being together when they could. They were not ready for marriage, however. "We're too young for it right now," Singleton said. "Tyra's definitely too young."[23]

Although marriage was not something they considered, Singleton said he was committed to dating only Banks. While walking in New York City, in front of the Empire State Building, Banks agreed to Singleton's request to date only him. "It sounds so corny," Singleton said. "But it's real."[24] Singleton also showed his feelings for Banks by throwing a surprise twentieth birthday party for her on a yacht. For her twenty-first birthday, Singleton gave her a sapphire and diamond ring. "Usually when you are with a girl, you begin to want to have your own space," Singleton said. "It's not like that with Tyra."[25]

Higher Learning

After Banks and Singleton began dating, Singleton urged Banks to try out for a part in his movie *Higher Learning*. He knew how hard she worked and thought she would be the perfect person to play Deja, the girlfriend of the main character in *Higher Learning*. Although he thought Banks would be great for the role, he did not automatically give her the part. He wanted her to read for the

Banks dedicated herself to the role of Deja in the movie Higher Learning.

role, but Banks initially hesitated to go through with the audition process. She did not want people to think she got her first movie role only because she and Singleton were a couple. "At first I felt that everyone would think I got the part because John is my boyfriend," she said. "But I do have talent as an actress, so eventually I decided the part was right for me. Sometimes it's very difficult because I have to balance two very stressful careers."[26]

Banks hoped to further her career as an actress beyond the television work she had done on *Fresh Prince*, and a part in a feature film would be a great opportunity for her. She ultimately decided to audition and succeeded. After she got the part, she was both nervous and excited about her first film role. She knew she had work ahead of her as she prepared for her first big-screen acting job. She was happy to find a good role, and her upbeat character brought optimism to the life of her on-screen boyfriend played by Omar Epps. Banks liked playing a smart and strong woman, a character who had more sense than her boyfriend.

Banks did not take her work as an actress for granted; instead she carefully prepared for the role. Her character was an athlete; so to look more like Deja, Banks trained for five weeks for four hours a day with the track coach from UCLA. She was in pain after falling while learning to do the hurdles, and she developed tendonitis in her ankles from the intense workout schedule, but did not quit. A body double had to be used in the movie for the hurdling scenes, but Banks nailed the clever and outgoing aspects of her character's personality. She eventually became so comfortable playing Deja that during filming that she ad-libbed a scene in which Deja critiqued her boyfriend's term paper.

Below Expectations

Singleton had lofty ambitions for *Higher Learning* as he looked to make a movie that made a statement about racial and sexual issues. The movie, which was released in 1995, dealt with tensions on a college campus. It received fair reviews but was not a blockbuster. More had been expected from Singleton in the wake of his success with *Boyz in the Hood*.

Rolling Stone magazine gave Singleton credit for trying to make a movie that made a difference. However, the magazine said the resulting movie tried to take on too much and did not always make sense. "Singleton can't begin to weave the disparate elements of his tragic fable into a coherent whole. Higher Learning is often cliched, unfocused and didactic," the magazine said.[27]

The film's characters behaved predictably, reviewer Richard Schickel commented in *Time* magazine, and stated that, although Singleton tried hard to make a statement with the film, the result was not an entertaining story. "Singleton has made all the right political moves," Schickel said, but added, "he hasn't really made a movie of them."[28] In the *New York Times*, Janet Maslin said Singleton did a good job of casting the movie, including his choice of Banks to play Deja. "Mr. Singleton assembles a cast of appealing actors who often fight the limitations of his two-dimensional screenplay," she said. "Tyra Banks brings obvious glamour to the role of his track-star girlfriend."[29]

The movie Banks and Singleton had made together was a disappointment, and off-screen their romance fizzled as well. Soon after *Higher Learning* was released in 1995, they were no longer a couple. The two were soon seeing other people, and the following year Singleton married actress Akosua Busia. Banks became romantically involved with Grammy-Award-winning singer Seal, but kept their relationship low profile.

Making History

While Banks kept her private life low key, her career was anything but subdued. In 1996 the twenty-two-year-old Banks made history as the first African American to appear on the cover of the *Sports Illustrated* swimsuit issue. The models do not know during the photo shoot which one will be featured on

Banks poses with the 1997 Sports Illustrated swimsuit issue, featuring her on the cover.

the cover, so learning that her photo had been chosen for the premier spot was an emotional experience for Banks. "When they announced it, I was totally crying in front of all of the cameras, and I felt really embarrassed. I was fine until one of the interviewers asked me, 'So how does it feel to be the first black woman on the cover?' and it just kind of freaked me out."[30]

Banks was not the only model on the cover that year. She posed in a leopard-spotted bikini alongside white model Valeria Mazza from Argentina. Banks was also featured inside the magazine in solo shots taken in South Africa. The 1996 cover was a historic move for the magazine, which had never used a woman of color on the cover of its popular swimsuit issue before. The move proved to be a profitable one for the magazine. The issue sold so well that they again chose Banks for the cover of the swimsuit issue the following year. On the cover of the 1997 issue, Banks was alone. She wore a pink bikini with white polka dots on a beach in the Bahamas, and the increased popularity of the swimsuit issue that year proved that she was the right model for the job.

Supermodel Stardom

Banks was making a name for herself as a well-known model and more. In addition to appearing on the highly visible *Sports Illustrated* covers, she also became the first black model on the cover of *GQ* magazine. She appeared in advertisements for commercial giants McDonald's, Coors, and Nike, and modeled lingerie for Victoria's Secret.

Banks earned $4 million a year from her Victoria's Secret contract and could earn $50,000 a day as a model. She may have been heavier than some of the other models and too curvy for high fashion, but she had a look and attitude that could sell. "When she walked down the [Victoria's Secret] runway, she was bigger than all the other girls, but if you asked anyone who their favorite was, it was always Tyra, because she's curvy," says Victoria's secret model Heidi Klum. "She hid the body parts she didn't want to show, and she rocked it."[31]

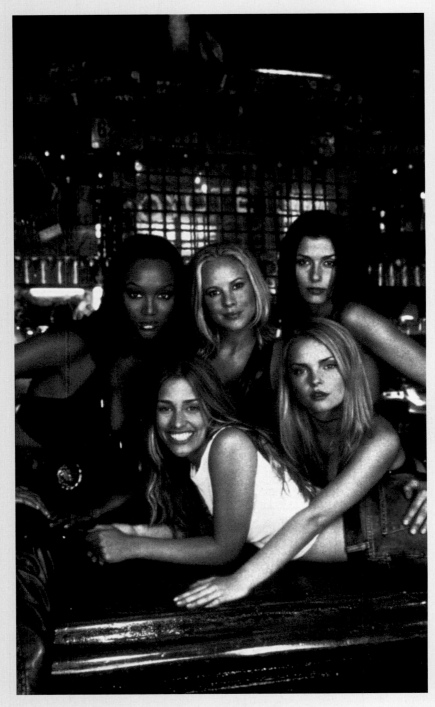

Banks, left, had a supporting role in the movie Coyote Ugly.

A Goofy Side

Tyra Banks and Heidi Klum were both models for Victoria's Secret and got along well. One thing that drew Klum and Banks together was their realization that fashion was not a life or death business. They acted silly when they needed to relieve tension and loosen things up on the runway.

Banks was serious about her job, but off the runway she acted more goofy than sexy. When she tried to talk in a low, sultry voice for her answering machine, she noticed that she could not pull it off. She was a hard worker but did not worry about maintaining a high-fashion look when she was not on the runway. She had a more casual look, and, when she was not modeling, did not always wear makeup or even comb her hair.

In 1997 she received the Michael Award for Supermodel of the Year, and Victoria's Secret chose her to model a $3 million bra. "Tyra Banks is on top of the world—her world, the fashion world and the world of entertainment, and she is still expanding. Her ascent to fame and to the status of being the most visible African-American model in the world this year has been astonishing," said *Ebony* magazine.[32]

Banks also continued her acting career. She was in the television series *Undercover* and had a small role in the 2002 Horror film *Halloween Resurrection*. She had a larger supporting role in the 2000 movie *Coyote Ugly,* a film about an aspiring songwriter, played by Piper Perabo, who travels to New York to find work and ends up getting a job at a bar.

Looking Ahead

Banks had reached a new level in her career. No longer simply a model, she was a budding actress and supermodel who nabbed the highest-profile commercial jobs. Banks was not only

Banks's curves and confidence made her a favorite amongst Victoria's Secret models and fans.

a good-looking model, but a smart one as well. She developed a wide range of expressions that she delivered as she walked down the runway or posed in front of the camera. She changed her demeanor from fierce to alluring simply by altering her smile. In addition, she knew how to hide her flaws. She might wear a little bit of material on the back of her bikini or alter a pose to take attention away from an area she did not want the camera to see.

She was on top of the modeling world, but she knew it was a position she would not hold for long. Modeling is a business that demands a certain look from its stars, and as she aged her body would not continue to be exactly what people were looking for in a model. "My mom encouraged me to look at modeling like being an athlete: You have a limited number of years 'in the game' with attention on you," Banks said. "Then they move on to someone younger and hotter. I knew one day I wouldn't be the It Girl anymore and I'd better plan ahead."[33]

While she was still a superstar, Banks made the most of her opportunities. Whether she was modeling for a magazine cover, acting, or filming a commercial, she noticed all that was going on as she prepared to take the next step in her career. She tried to become familiar with the work behind the glamorous scenes, so she would be ready when the time came for her to step into a new role.

Banks was constantly looking at ways to reach beyond modeling for more opportunities and challenges. She looked up to supermodel Cindy Crawford, who was a businesswoman as well as a model. Banks admired the way Crawford took control of her career and had business ventures outside of modeling. Banks also wanted to move into businesses that used her name and experience as a selling point. "Even as a model I used to think 'brand,'" she said. "My mom always told me, 'Plan for the end at the beginning.'…I always looked at it knowing that there was something after."[34]

Her future plans were not concrete, but now that Banks had fame, she wanted to do something tangible with her success. She was aware that she had entered the spotlight because of her looks and tried to send the right message to young women who saw her in the media. She was concerned that the body image most rail-thin models projected was not a healthy one. To counter this, she set her sights on developing programs to boost the self-image of young women and teach them to be proud of who they are.

Chapter 4

Role Model and Mentor

Although she was a model, Banks knew her body was not perfect. She had endured criticism as a high-fashion model and learned to work around her imperfections. She never let comments about her looks keep her from moving on to another career opportunity. Now, her message emphasized that a person's success in life did not depend on the way they looked.

Although her looks were a big part of the reason she was famous, Banks delivered a message that contradicted the modeling industry's image of a perfect body. She let girls who admired her as a model know that there was more to life than trying to look beautiful. She aspired to impart that inner strength is more important than external beauty. "I feel like it's my responsibility to do something about [body image] because I was in fashion for so long projecting an image that's so hard to live up to," she said.[35]

The modeling, commercials, and acting that brought Banks fame and made her a nationally known figure also gave her the financial means and name recognition she needed to deliver her message. Banks used her popularity to let girls and young women know they had a great deal to offer no matter how they looked or dressed. She wrote a book aimed at teens, spoke at colleges, and founded a summer camp for girls.

Answering Questions

Banks was a successful, beautiful young woman, and girls felt comfortable turning to her for advice. She received letters from

Tyra Banks Scholarship Fund

It did not take Banks long to use the money she made in modeling to help others. In 1992, a year after she began modeling, Banks founded the Tyra Banks Scholarship Fund for African American children.

The scholarship fund supported something Banks believed in: education. She wanted others to graduate from high school and created a high school scholarship fund for her old school, Immaculate Heart High School.

teens and pre-teens asking for help with their problems, including boy troubles and weight concerns. Banks could not reach each girl personally, but looked for a way to do something that would let these girls know that she cared and had information and experience to share.

To get in touch with her audience, in 1998 she wrote *Tyra's Beauty Inside & Out* with Vanessa Thomas Bush. The self-help book was geared toward teens and addressed skin care, hair, makeup, and fashion. The book was more than a guide to looking good and applying eyeliner, however, it also addressed weightier topics such as alcohol and drugs, and offered life lessons, such as advice on relationships and self esteem. Banks shared personal stories about her childhood and friendship troubles and also talked about the pain she felt for months when a relationship ended. She told humorous and embarrassing stories about her life as a model, such as the time she was in a store's fitting room and a saleswoman opened the door when she was wearing nothing but her underwear. "Wow, it really is Tyra Banks!" the woman exclaimed.[36]

Banks admitted that she was not perfect, that she could be bossy, blunt, and too silly at times, but added that she

Tyra's Beauty Inside and Out *gave advice on fashion, as well as relationships and self-esteem.*

had learned to be confident and to deal with her issues. She ended the book on an upbeat note, encouraging girls to think positively about themselves. Banks wanted her readers to have dreams for their future and to feel that they could do anything. "Young folks should feel positive about themselves," she said. "They should create goals for their lives, and work hard to make their dreams come true."[37]

TZONE

When Banks was on tours promoting her book, girls often asked her for advice. Listening to their questions led to another project for Banks. To further her work with girls and become an active mentor, she founded the TZONE camp in Southern California. The week-long summer camp for teens offered activities for girls from varied backgrounds and gave them the opportunity to build self-esteem and leadership skills as they learned to deal with people from a variety of backgrounds. "I handpick a diverse group of girls, not only of different cultures but also life experiences and economic backgrounds," Banks said. "We structure the program so they can really learn from each other."[38]

Banks wanted the campers to be proud of who they were. Many girls looked up to her because she was a model, and she wanted to let them know that they did not have to look perfect to be a worthy person. "It's my responsibility to tear down the wall between who young women think they should be and who they really are," she said.[39]

Banks took an active role in the camps, working directly with the girls she had been hearing from. She read the essays from girls who applied for the camp and chose girls who needed help, especially those dealing with issues such as drug use, poverty, or abusive parents. At the camp she was part of discussions on topics such as diversity, insecurity, and lifestyle choices as well as appearance. She even led the group in cheers such as, "My sister! My sister! I got your back."[40] Banks wanted to tell young girls that it was the qualities that they had inside that would bring them success. "What I tell the girls is that all the insecurities we have, we can't let those defeat us," she said. "We've got to keep on keepin' on."[41]

The girls at the camp also participated in other activities, such as a challenging ropes course and improvisational comedy. At night they might meet around the campfire for a "lemon squeezer"[42] session that Banks said squeezed out everyone's emotions and gave the girls an opportunity to talk about issues. To help them understand that everyone goes through difficult times,

Banks shared her personal stories of youthful insecurity with the campers. "I tell the girls of my experiences growing up—how it was difficult for me, too," she says. "A lot of them are shocked when they see me shed tears about the things I'm not happy with about myself."[43]

Banks wanted to erase self-doubt and have girls support each other. Her goal to help adolescents stemmed in part from the fact that she had been teased as a teen because of her looks. She wanted these girls to feel good about themselves because

Achieving the Look

Banks's self-assured and approachable personality set her apart from other supermodels. She consistently went against the aloof and cool image of models by admitting that she was not perfect. She did not wake up looking like a model, she said, and explained that achieving a fashionable look required hours of working with her hair and makeup.

She admitted that she wore hair extensions to make her hair look fuller and longer. Even the clothes she wore at fashion shoots did not fit her perfectly, she said. A small shirt might be cut in back to make it look as if it fit. A large shirt was pulled tight with safety pins. She made it clear that the perfect images of her that young women saw in magazines were not what she looked like in real life.

Banks credited her success as a model to her ability to capture a pose and to show off her best looks. She was a top model not only because of her natural good looks, but because she worked to figure out how to best use her natural beauty. "Believe it or not, I just really know how to pose well," she said. "It took me five years to learn what my best angles are."

Lynn Norment, "Tyra Banks: On Top of the World," *Ebony*, May 1997, p. 110.

Banks spending time with girls from her TZONE camp, which focuses on self-empowerment and supporting others.

she knew what it was like to feel like an outcast. "At camp we talk about things like mean girls and cliques and how the problem can continue into adulthood," she said. "I want girls to know that being picked on seems horrible right now, but it really is going to get better. I'm living proof. You're going to get out of the hell you're in right now. It's usually the gawky girls, or the ones who are overweight or too skinny or too nerdy, who turn into swans."[44]

Banks realized that the teens' need for improved self-images extended beyond what she could do with the camp. She could help a few hundred girls with her hands-on approach at TZONE, so to assist others she set up a foundation that gave money to other organizations that helped disadvantaged girls. When she became too consumed by other business ventures to stay involved with details such as choosing the girls for camp, her TZONE Foundation allowed Banks to continue to help and to extend her reach beyond Southern California to help organizations for girls across the United States.

Life Size

Banks increased her appeal to teens and pre-teens by acting in the movie *Life Size* in 2000. The Disney channel movie aimed at teens and preteens was about a doll who comes to life to fulfill the wish of a young girl, played by Lindsay Lohan. Lohan's character had lost her mother, and she wishes for her mother to return to life. The spell goes awry, and a doll named Eve, played by Banks, comes to life instead.

The movie gave Banks the opportunity to show off her ability to do light comedy. The ever-confident Eve tries to work as a secretary, but has no idea what she is doing, and she makes comments about fashion at the wrong time. Banks plays Eve with a naïve and sweet personality, while Lohan counters with a smart and worldly portrayal of the girl who brings Eve to life and is sometimes frustrated by Eve's childlike nature. The combination made for a likeable movie that entertained its audience.

The Inside Scoop on Tyra

While promoting her book, *Beauty Inside and Out*, Tyra did interviews with the press. During one interview, she explained that she enjoyed modeling because it gave her control over her time. The media also asked how she handled the men who were interested in her because of her appearance on the *Sports Illustrated* cover. "I wish the 'right' men would approach me," she said. "Being Daddy's lil' girl, I know how to pick and choose the men around me."

When it was time for her to relax after a long day, Tyra said that she chose a warm bath, jogging, and watching television. Her passion, however, involved food. "I love to eat and cook spaghetti," she admitted.

Renee Minus White, "Tyra Tips off Teens with New Beauty Book," *New Amsterdam News,* April 9, 1998, p. 17.

Down-to-earth Supermodel

Banks's interest in making movies for teens, and sponsoring programs for them, may have been surprising for a high-paid, high-profile fashion model, but Banks had a down-to-earth side to her personality. She may have been known for her looks and her curvy figure, but that was not how she saw herself. She identified more with typical twenty-year-olds than superstars. "I see myself as I am before the hair-and-makeup person arrives: a normal girl who could blend in walking down the street," she said. "All this makeup and the person I become in front of the camera when it's 'showtime' have nothing to do with who I am in any real way."[45]

Banks did not act like a superstar, and in some ways she did not live a superstar life. When her swimsuit photos were featured in her own calendar in 1997, the publisher had the idea of kicking it off with a star-studded party. Banks had a difficult time thinking of stars she knew well enough to invite. The *Sports Illustrated* model turned to professional athletes to help her promote the calendar and was happy to have NBA players such as Scottie Pippen at the calendar's launch party.

Talk Show Correspondent

Banks may have struggled to fill the guest list for her party, but she was not struggling in her career. She had the calendar, book, acting, camp, and foundation to keep her busy as well as her continuing modeling career. In 1999 she added another job title to her resume: talk show correspondent.

Banks broadened her media experience with help from the biggest name in daytime talk shows, Oprah Winfrey. She had the title of "youth correspondent" for *The Oprah Winfrey Show* and was thrilled with the opportunity to work with Winfrey. She considered the talk show host a mentor and made some appearances on her show for a few seasons, doing makeovers and introducing her mother.

Banks enjoyed her regular appearances on *The Oprah Winfrey Show* and was offered her own talk show in 2001. A producer

Tyra became a youth correspondent for The Oprah Winfrey Show and admired Oprah's smart business sense.

was impressed by her demeanor and believed that as host of her own show she could attract a younger audience than Oprah. "She seemed wise beyond her years and I wasn't expecting that from a supermodel," said television show producer Hilary Estey McLoughlin. "I began to pursue Tyra about having her own talk show. I thought she could fill a void in the marketplace."[46]

Tyra turned down the opportunity. She was not yet ready to be in charge of her own talk show, and she had a few other things to try first.

A Mentor

Banks was positioning herself as a mentor for her generation and a role model for younger girls. As a correspondent for Oprah, an author, and an actress, as well as through running her camps and foundation, she was showing that she had an interest in the issues that mattered to women and girls. She had gained fame as a model, but rather than focusing attention only on outer beauty, she encouraged women and girls to work on their inner beauty as well.

Banks was always on the lookout for ways to further her career. She enjoyed acting, working in television, and mentoring young women. For her next project, she found a way to combine those three interests in a program that also built upon her fame and expertise as a supermodel.

Chapter 5

Top Model

Banks continued to support her TZONE foundation and remained concerned about issues relating to women and young girls, but she still had her modeling and acting careers to consider. She also kept modeling for Victoria's Secret and pursued her interest in working in television. She had ideas for taking her career in a new direction but did not sit back and wait for opportunities to come to her. The creative and determined model and businesswoman thought of ways to make things happen.

Banks's next big idea came to her in the kitchen while she was making tea. She devised an idea for a reality television show that would allow her to pass on her knowledge of the fashion industry to young, aspiring models. She wanted to combine her desire to be a role model to young women and take advantage of her knowledge of the fashion industry. In addition, a national television show would be a huge boost to her career.

Banks was aware that reality television shows had huge audiences, so she planned a show that followed a group of young women who were in a real-life competition to be a fashion model. She made the show's premise mesh with her principles of encouraging girls to be the best they could be and not relying on their looks to get them places. She intended to show her audience that modeling was as much about effort and hard work as it was looking good. She also looked at the show as a way to give girls a chance to realize a dream. "I wanted to do a show where people were striving for a goal, winning something that you've worked hard for," she said.[47]

Banks wanted to pass on her knowledge of the fashion industry and created America's Next Top Model.

Her idea for a modeling reality show became *America's Next Top Model*, a cross between a reality show and a modeling competition. It would offer insights on the modeling industry and focus on the drama that arose between the competitors. Banks knew her idea was a solid one, but now she had to find a way to get her show on the air.

Selling Her Idea

It was one thing for Banks to have an idea, and another for her to find a producer to help her put the show together. She had long been interested in movies and television, but it was difficult to get people to take her seriously as a television show producer. Although she had acting experience and was a successful model,

Selecting the Judges

When Tyra Banks put together the show *America's Next Top Model,* she not only had to choose contestants but judges as well. In the first season she asked former supermodels Janice Dickinson, Kimora Lee Simmons, and Beau Quillian to help her judge the contestants. "I might have been a little bit skeptical because that was in the beginning of reality TV," Simmons said. "But I would always do anything to help Tyra."

Banks also had her makeup artist Jay Manuel involved in the show, and she hired J. Alexander to teach the contestants how to walk. Manuel and Alexander eventually became judges on the show, and, when the first season was being filmed, Alexander had no idea that Banks's concept would turn out to be such a hit. "It was just another job," he said. "No one had any idea the show was going to get this big."

"'Model' Making," *Entertainment Weekly,* February 22, 2008, p. 34.

that did not mean she had an easy time convincing people she could be the force behind a television show. "As a model, my roadblock was being black and curvy," she said. "As a producer, my roadblock was being a model."[48]

Even her agent was initially skeptical about the show, but Banks eventually found someone interested in helping her get the program off the ground. Ken Mok, who was involved with the reality competition show *Making the Band*, became the executive producer of the series. He helped her turn her idea into a show and sell it to the UPN Network. He was impressed by Banks and backed her idea because he liked her drive and her plans for her career. "The minute you meet her, you understand why she's a supermodel," he said. "She has such a big-picture sense about herself."[49]

Taking Control

Once Banks found a producer for the show, she did not hand off her idea. She remained involved with the project as her idea evolved into a show. She did interviews on radio shows to get the word out that she was looking for aspiring models for a new television series and helped choose the girls who would be on the show. Banks and the production crew watched video after video of modeling hopefuls as Banks looked for girls who would make the show interesting and who had what it took to become a star. "We had tapes of thousands of gorgeous girls. But we'd watch the tapes and say, 'She's boring,' or 'She's conceited.' Beauty's easy. Modeling is not just about being pretty," Banks said.[50] Banks also made sure that the aspiring models on the show were not all the same size or ethnic background. She chose women with a variety of looks.

Over the course of eight weeks, the first season was filmed. The crew was working with a budget of $500,000, and to cut costs Banks used her own wardrobe to provide clothing for the contestants. She was concerned with every detail and, when the set was being built, even glued beads to it to give it the glamorous look she wanted.

Banks, model Paulina Porizkova, and J. Alexander, are the judges on how the girls performed on **America's Next Top Model.**

To show that modeling was about more than beauty, the program included a number of challenges for the contestants. To become *America's Next Top Model,* the group of aspiring young models had to live together and at the same time compete for a chance to win a lucrative modeling contract. Having the girls live with each other gave the show a dramatic edge as personality conflicts erupted. For the competition aspect of the show, the aspiring models participated in challenges involving modeling, and Banks and a panel of celebrity judges commented on their performances.

The young models were the main focus of the show, but Banks was clearly the one in charge of this production. Banks positioned herself as the fashion guru that the girls needed to impress. Her image appeared everywhere on the show. There were pictures of her in the home where the girls lived, and they received messages from her (called "Tyra Mail") and competed in challenges she helped devise. She was the lead judge on the show as well as critic, mentor, and friend to the girls competing for the prize. She was the one who could let the girls into the world of high fashion and glamour, and it was up to the modeling hopefuls to impress her.

Personal Interest

For the show's first season, which premiered in summer 2003, ten girls were chosen to live in a New York apartment building and compete for a modeling deal. They struggled to get along together as they learned the finer points of modeling. On a chilly day they faced their first challenge: doing a swimsuit photo shoot on top of a Manhattan skyscraper. Banks and a group of fashion experts judged the models' photos, and then the models were called in to face Banks and the others. One by one Banks talked about their flaws and strengths until only two models were left. The first one eliminated was a young modeling hopeful who fumbled her footing on the runway. After she left, the others tried to prove that they were worthy of the prize. Each week the contestants faced a different challenge, including visiting modeling agencies, doing a photo that involved movement, and being asked to do a nude photo shoot. Even the elimination room scene could be a challenge, because it sometimes took as long as five hours to film.

Banks and the other judges looked for more than nice photos as they sought to find a girl who could be a successful model. One girl was criticized for consistently looking for compliments, as Banks emphasized that modeling is more than looking good and being admired by others. The life of a model is not always glamorous, and Banks made that clear to the contestants and viewers. "Too many girls go in thinking that it's all about glamour and being fine and having a ton of makeup on and trying to be Miss Sexpot," she said. "That ain't gonna work. Not at all."[51]

Enthusiastic Model

When Banks was making the first seasons of the show *America's Top Model,* she not only taught young women to become models, she continued to work in the industry herself. In November 2003 she appeared in the annual Victoria's Secret fashion show with other models such as Heidi Klum, Gisele Bundchen, and Naomi Campbell.

She was relaxed and confident as she prepared for the show, although preparing was not simple. It took the models eight hours to get ready for the one-hour show, but Tyra was not frustrated. As the show neared she was excited to get on the runway. Rather than being nervous, she was eager to get onstage. "To me, the stage, lights, action mean 'bring it, girl!'" she said.

Donna Freydkin, "Heavenly Bodies' 'Secret' Exposed," *USA Today,* November 19, 2003, p. 06d.

Banks's goal for the aspiring models to grow during their time on the show and looked to make the program a life-changing experience for them. She wanted all the models who competed to learn from the challenges they faced. After a model was eliminated from the show, Banks went and talked to her, sometimes for hours. Rather than have a contestant leave with a feeling of being defeated, Banks tried to soothe the girl's feelings and make her feel confident again.

Successful Format

America's Next Top Model was first shown in summer 2003 on the UPN network, a small, new network that eventually became the CW network. Although *America's Next Top Model* did not appear on a major network, the show still gathered a significant following because it provided entertainment and also gave viewers insights

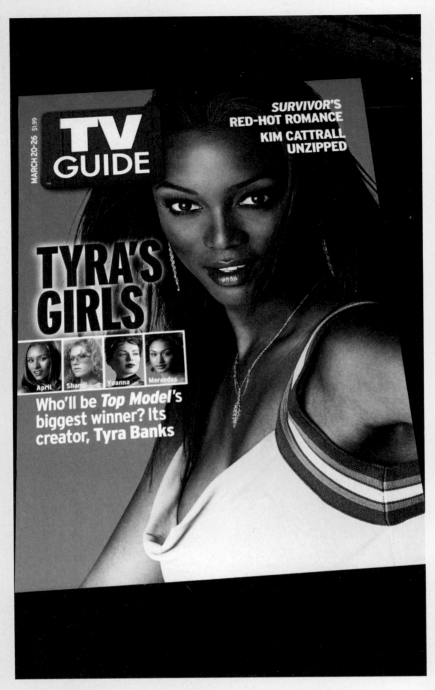

America's Next Top Model *became a huge hit with national attention.*

into the modeling industry. The personality conflicts between the models became one of the show's focal points, and the challenges the models competed in were interesting because viewers wondered how the contestants would manage the tasks they faced. At the end of the first season, contestants Adrianne Curry, Shannon Stewart, and Elyse Sewell remained to compete in the final show. Sewell was eliminated first, and Adrianne and Shannon faced off in the final challenge, a runway fashion show with professional models. In the end Adrianne was chosen because of her edgy looks. Adrianne commented that she was sure her win would

Not Successful at Everything

Banks had a successful show and remained a popular model, but in 2004 she tried another new venture that failed. She had thoughts of launching a singing career and hired Benny Medina to be her manager. He was Mariah Carey's music manager and had also worked with Jennifer Lopez. She paid $30,000 to make a video for the song "Shake Ya Body," which was shown on an episode of *America's Next Top Model.*

She hoped to land a record deal after making the song but could see that she was taking a chance. She might fail, but she was not afraid to try. "I know I could fall on my face, but that's life," she said. "I'm not going to let that stop me."

The song was posted on the UPN Web site and received 155,000 hits. Record companies failed, however, to show interest in signing Banks to a contract. It became clear to her that she was not a great singer. "That was a dream," she said when she looked back on her singing efforts a few years later. "I sounded decent, but you shouldn't ever do something just because you're only decent at it."

Marc Peyser and Allison Samuels, "The Tyra Typhoon," *Newsweek,* March 22, 2004, p. 10.

Kiri Blakeley, "Tyra Banks on It," *Forbes,* July 3, 2006, p. 120.

change her life, which it did. She appeared on the VH1 reality show *The Surreal Life*, married former child star Christopher Knight, modeled for magazines, and appeared on television and in movies.

By its second season, the show was the top-rated program for the UPN Network. Although it didn't attract as many viewers as shows on the major networks did, it did pull in more than 7 million viewers at times. It was popular with viewers ages eighteen to thirty-four, at times cracking the top twenty-five shows for that age group in a given week.

Banks knew how popular the show was becoming from the reaction she got from fans. When fans recognized her in public, they did not ask for her autograph but rather what was going to happen on the show. After the show's successful first season, or cycle, people in the modeling industry who had initially been skeptical about *America's Top Model* now were won over, Banks said. Supermodels, including Gisele Bundchen, supported it. "Gisele Bundchen was raving about the show," Banks says. "We just had a Victoria's Secret appearance at a store in New York. She was yelling to the press, 'Her show is the best thing in the world. You have to watch it.'"[52]

New Directions

The success of the first season gave Banks the opportunity to make the show even edgier the next season. She shot the first episode on an aircraft carrier, and later in the cycle asked the contestants to pose wearing nothing but body paint. "The first season I was nervous about making it too edgy in terms of the photo shoots," Banks said. "This season we're going to do high fashion, the kind of fashion people are going to love or hate or not understand."[53]

The show, which aired spring 2004, was again a success. Banks had been initially uncertain if the show would even make it through one season, but now looked forward to many more *Top Model* cycles. By the end of its third cycle in 2004, the show was winning its time period for viewers age eighteen to thirty-four and was the UPN network's shining star. "*Top model* has been incredible for UPN," noted television analyst Carolyn Finger, "It's their one show that universally it can be said any network would like to have."[54]

With the success of *America's Next Top Model*, Banks considered developing more television shows. She thought about starring in and producing a movie, and considered developing her own line of lingerie or establishing an Internet community. As Banks decided where to focus her energy next, she sometimes felt a little lost. She had no map to follow for what she was doing, but there was no doubt that she planned to keep moving. "I want to be successful across the board," Banks said. "I want an empire like Oprah's."[55]

Chapter 6

Talk Show Star

As Banks tried to decide where next to take her career, an issue in her personal life pointed her in the right direction. Banks had been dating a person who repeatedly cheated on her. When she forgave him and took him back, he cheated on her again. Finally, she ended the relationship, even though it broke her heart. The break-up was an emotionally painful experience for Banks, but it gave her a connection to other women who had been through similar situations.

This experience helped Banks decide to pursue her own daytime talk show. A few years earlier she had considered a talk show but felt she was too inexperienced. Now she was more savvy about the television industry and less judgmental of others than she had been when she was younger. She felt emotionally stronger and ready to impart her wisdom to a daytime audience. "I think a lot of women of my generation are afraid of being vulnerable," she said. "Well, that's what we're going to explore on my show."[56]

Banks saw herself as a voice for her generation. The mistakes she had made in her relationship and the pain from the breakup helped her relate to other women who had experienced a broken heart. "That relationship made me smarter and made me a great talk show host," Banks said. "When I was in it, I was miserable. But without him, I couldn't sit on this couch with my guests and feel their painful stories with them. Now I get what they're going through."[57]

Right for Daytime?

Not everyone believed that Banks would be a success at her new venture. She was well known as a supermodel and a frank judge on *America's Next Top Model*, but few knew of her dedication and work behind the scenes of her show. Many questioned

Banks wanted to reach out to her generation more and pushed to launch her own talk show.

whether she had the right look for a talk show. "Despite her track record with *Model* and her frequent appearances on *The Oprah Winfrey Show*, people are wondering whether she has the goods to conquer daytime talk, a crowded market that tends to embrace plainer-looking hosts, not gorgeous supermodels," noted writer Christopher Lisotta.[58]

Despite those who wondered about her ability to be a daytime talk show host, Banks was confident the show would work. She had been questioned when she created the TZONE summer camp and the *Top Model* show, and those projects had been successful. With her latest venture, she felt she had the right combination of experience and personality to pull off her show, and her producer had faith in her. "When you really look at her, she defies expectations," said Jim Paratore, president of Telepictures Productions. "She's a very real, relatable, open person. And she's a hands-on producer. She will be the driver of this show as well."[59]

Paratore noted that Banks's work with *Top Model* had brought female viewers to the fledgling UPN network. Her ability to encourage young women to tune in and watch would be a plus with her daytime talk show. Dick Robertson, a Warner Brothers executive, believed that women who were in her target audience of eighteen to forty-nine years old would be interested in hearing what Banks had to say. "She's extremely smart, very grounded and also easy on the eyes," he said. "We think she's got the talk show goods to pull this off."[60]

The Tyra Banks Show

Banks's talk show premiered in September 2005. In addition to interviewing celebrity guests such as Beyoncé and Nicole Richie, she also talked to ordinary people about their personal issues. Banks played against the aloof supermodel stereotype by being very open and down to earth with her guests. This helped her establish a friendly connection with her audience, showing that she was as real as she was beautiful. She was not afraid to act goofy or clown around. Banks saw the show more as a way to share information than a traditional talk show. "It's a woman's guide to life," she said. "It's topical, connected to the news, but we do fashion and fun stuff.

Banks was open and relaxed with her guests, including 2008 presidential candidate Barack Obama.

It's like different pages or sections in a women's magazine. They're unique, but they all fit together under one cover."[61]

Banks, determined to make her show succeed and to draw viewers, did not hold back from revealing information about herself or pulling off stunts that generated publicity. She showed her audience how her photos were retouched for magazines to make her look thinner and admitted that she used hair extensions and false eyelashes. She explained that a push-up bra exaggerated the size of her breasts and also addressed a rumor that she had had breast implants. "It's something that a lot of the public...think that I have, and that's so frustrating for me," she said.[62] To prove that her breasts were real, a doctor came onto the program, did a sonogram, and said that her breasts were natural.

To bring in viewers Banks also interviewed her former modeling nemesis Naomi Campbell to put their feud to rest and did some flamboyant social experiments, such as wearing a fat suit and going undercover as a homeless person and a stripper. Banks connected with her audience by showing a vulnerable side to her personality and followed her value of getting women to empower each other by creating a "Sisterhood Initiative" for her show. She designed it to bring women closer together and to encourage them to find the good in each other rather than the negative. Banks wanted her show to make a positive impact as

Openly Imperfect

One thing that strengthened Banks's appeal was her willingness to admit that she had flaws. The supermodel was open about her imperfections. She talked about having a fear of dolphins on her talk show and even admitted that photos of her were touched up to take off the cellulite. "I disappoint people who meet me in person because I don't look like me," Banks said. "But the public is really hard on people in the industry, and your image has to be perfect, and I openly admit that I have cellulite and I get that touched off."

Banks also admitted that she was jealous of talk show giant Oprah Winfrey. Banks had said that she did not envy Winfrey, but, when she took a lie detector test on an episode of *The Tyra Banks Show*, the test showed that the jealousy did indeed exist. When the results were revealed, Banks laughed and admitted that she did want some of the things that Oprah had. "Well she's really rich, c'mon! I want 500 million dollars," Banks said. "I want the money, I want the house in Santa Barbara, the big condo in Chicago. I want the girl's school in Africa, the gorgeous hair!"

Donna Freydkin "Doctored Cover Photos Add Up to Controversy," *USA Today,* June 17, 2003, p. 03d.

"Lie Detector Proves Tyra Banks Is Jealous of Oprah," *The Celebrity Truth,* February 6, 2008, http://www.thecelebritytruth.com/lie-detector-proves-tyra-banks-is-jealous-of-oprah

well as provide entertainment. "I want the show to be as real as possible," she said. "I don't want fluff."[63]

Mixed Reviews

Despite her attempt to create a show that would appeal to every woman, Banks's talk show had both fans and detractors. Some liked the way she identified with the women in her audience and how she played against her good looks. Others felt her show lacked content and that she was cheapening her image with stunts to generate publicity for the show. Although the show was building a base of viewers, it was not as well-received immediately as *America's Top Model* had been. "The trouble is, *Tyra* is often beneath Tyra," *People* magazine said. "She fares better in segments that exploit her penchant for keepin' it real—stripping off her makeup was a nice touch—though she often struggles to fill the hour."[64]

Banks did not get defensive about the criticism of her show, but took it to heart and worked to make improvements. She learned how to interact more comfortably with her guests and became a better listener when doing interviews. "In year one I was tentative and still feeling my way into the job," she said. "I remember thinking more about what I was going to ask and not listening as much as I could. In year two I'm more confident in my instincts and sure of the direction of the show. I really listen to my guests and their questions, and it's more of a conversation and exchange of ideas."[65]

Despite the criticism, Banks put effort into her new venture and had the support of her network and producers. She was working hard to produce a creative and interesting show. She was even called a young Oprah at times, but she felt intimidated rather than flattered at this comparison. She did not want to try to measure up to the talk show mogul. Watching Oprah's show, which she admired, inspired her to make improvements on her own program. "The first season I was 40 percent happy with my show. I was not 100 percent happy," she told interviewer Greta Van Susteren. "I'd watch

Dual Image

Banks developed one image for *Top Model* and another for *The Tyra Banks Show*. To make *Top Model* entertaining, she created a fierce version of herself and acted demanding and critical of the contestants. On *The Tyra Banks Show*, she was friendly, open, and vulnerable. She admitted her faults and chatted candidly with her guests.

Banks admitted that the *Top Model* version of herself was more of a character and that part of the reason for her sharp remarks was a need to make the show interesting. On her talk show her real personality could come through, although she admitted that her glamorous look took hours of hair and makeup preparation. She described her two images as the daytime Tyra and the nighttime Tyra. "The Daytime Tyra is who I am," she said. "I'm tough sometimes, I'm warm, I'm uplifting women. That's my cause, that's my 'why I think I'm here'—to do that."

Nancy Jo Sales, "A Model Mogul," *Vanity Fair,* February 2007, p. 168.

my show. Then I'd watch 'Oprah.' And I'd be like, oh my God, we are just a mess. We were such a mess."[66] Rather than becoming distracted by the comparisons and feeling her show fell short when compared to Oprah's, Banks looked at how she could be a better talk show host and how her program could be improved. Banks aspired to be authentic and unpretentious like Oprah, and worked to live up to the daytime talk show standard Oprah set.

Demanding Schedule

Banks worked hard to connect with her audience, often going online to check popular topics of the day to weave into her show. She visited her show's Web site to read feedback from viewers. The

Banks worked incessantly on her shows—promoting them and working behind the scenes.

improvements to the show made a difference, and *The Tyra Banks Show* was nominated for six Daytime Emmy Awards in 2007, including ones for outstanding show and host. "The nomination was a surprise to me and I was thrilled!" she said. "I was on cloud nine for a week after I learned about the nomination. I always knew this is what I wanted to do, and the nomination is validation of that ambition."[67]

Banks was heavily involved in making The *The Tyra Banks Show* the best it could be as she looked to be both girlfriend and role model to her viewers. She was a hands-on producer, not a celebrity who put her name on a project but remained aloof. "I've spent sleepless nights and countless hours behind the scenes," she noted.

> There's the amount of time you see me onscreen, and I'm spending at least three times that amount behind the scenes. I need to be involved in everything, from the [graphics] to Web design and content, props and production—and show content, of course. I have an incredible team of devoted people who help create and build my vision and take it to that next level."[68]

While she kept up with the details of her talk show, Banks remained producer of *America's Next Top Model,* sending e-mails to her staff in the middle of the night if she had an idea or feared something was going wrong. Banks put in long days as she contributed to thirteen weekly episodes of *Top Model* every six months and recorded two talk shows a day between August and December. Her schedule was a tiring one, but Banks was a perfectionist who wanted everything to go right on both shows.

Banks saw her demanding schedule as a necessary part of her desire to build a strong business. She was no longer simply a model or actress, but a businesswoman focused on her work and responsible for the success of a number of projects. She did not lend her name to a show to boost its popularity. She made sure the projects she was involved in were the best they could be and that she had a significant say in how things were done. "As a model, I had a reputation of a woman who was on time and was

Dedication Yes, Manicure No

Working on a talk show and a reality show meant that Banks had less time to polish her appearance. She admitted it was tough to keep herself looking top-notch while she was so busy making the shows. She did not even have time for a manicure. She did not mind, however, giving up some of her polished looks for the chance to be in control of her own television shows.

When she was in the middle of creating a television show, Banks even gave up sleeping and free time to make sure it was a success. She likened the experience to being the parent of a newborn. "You don't sleep when you have a new baby," she said. "I didn't sleep. I didn't have weekends. I worked nonstop. You wouldn't let just anybody baby-sit your child. When I hire someone, I have to feel that I connect with them as a person. I'm looking for honest people. I'm looking for loyalty. I'm looking for people who respect people at all levels, from people who clean the building to the people who own the building."

Tyra Banks et al., "What Matters Most in My Work and My Life," *Newsweek,* October 20, 2008, p. 54.

very businesslike and didn't party," she explained. "So now I have to build my reputation to [have others] say, 'She works 24/7, she has tunnel vision, she doesn't put her name on vanity projects.' I think that is starting to be seen, but it takes time."[69]

Taking Its Toll

It was not easy for Banks to manage both shows, and her busy schedule took its toll. Lack of sleep affected her mood, and, during the fourth season of *Top Model*, she lashed out at a contestant for not taking the competition seriously enough. "I was rooting for you! We were all rooting for you! How dare you!...You rolling your eyes and you act like you heard it all before," she said to the girl. "You have no idea what I been through. But I'm not a victim! I grow from it and I learn!"[70] As the other models watched the outburst with frightened looks on their faces, the girl broke down in tears.

Tyra's outburst was not unnoticed by critics. *Entertainment Weekly's* Tim Stack rated her meltdown a five on a strength scale of one to five, calling it a case of "Diva Rage." Stack described the incident this way: "In a display of un-model behavior, Tyra launches into a Naomi Campbell-style tirade when Tiffany shows no emotion after getting voted off."[71] Banks later addressed the issue and admitted that the incident occurred because she was exhausted. She also noted that she reacted strongly because she was emotionally invested in the contestants and cared about what they did with their lives. She wanted to see them become better people. "I felt like I created this show, I plucked this girl out of her obscure life and put her here, and it is my responsibility to make sure that she's successful," she said.[72]

Although she felt responsible for the well-being of the young women on her show, Banks came to the conclusion that something had to change. She had been talking to each contestant dropped from the show, but decided that was best left to the show's therapists. She could not be everywhere and had to delegate more oversight to the people who worked for her. For her own good, she had to detach herself emotionally from the contestants.

Banks pulled back from some of the work behind the scenes, but remained visible on the show. The contestants still received "Tyra Mail" with instructions for their next assignment, and Banks remained one of the show's judges. The show kept pulling in viewers and was shown in 110 countries. "No hour of TV provides more of an escape than Tyra Banks's brilliantly executed reality competition..." *People* magazine said. "Beyond the fantasy fulfillment—the gorgeous getups, the catwalk strutting—is a briskly paced series stuffed to the seams with creative new challenges."[73]

Goodbye to Modeling

In addition to cutting down her involvement with *Top Model*, Banks decided it was time to retire from modeling. When she first began working on *Top Model* and her talk show, Banks still modeled occasionally for companies such as Victoria's Secret. At age thirty-two, however, she decided it was time to say goodbye to that part of her career.

Banks left modeling in 2006, before it became obvious she was past her prime in that line of work. She had plenty of other projects to occupy her time and did not want people looking at her and wondering why she was still clinging to the runway.

To lessen her workload and focus on her shows Banks quit modeling.

"I felt like it was important to walk away while you're still on top," she said, "and not be walking down the Victoria's Secret runway and your booty's jiggling, and it's like 'What is she doing? Do something else.'"[74]

Successful Businesswoman

Banks no longer needed to model for financial reasons because she was successful in her other ventures. Forbes estimated she earned more than $18 million in 2005 and in 2006. Her own company, Bankable Productions, owned her talk show, and she was looking to produce other television programs as well.

Model and friend Heidi Klum was not surprised by Banks's success. "She's one of the most hardworking people I know—I've seen her go straight from a late night of press to an early-morning shoot with no complaints,"[75] Klum said. Klum added that Banks was both passionate about her work and compassionate with her coworkers. "Her appeal is obvious to anyone who knows her, whether personally or professionally or just from her shows," she said. "She is dynamic, positive and real, and we are only at the beginning of her special brand of global domination."[76]

Banks had clearly found her niche in television as she built upon her career as a supermodel to create and star in two successful programs. Her famous name drew attention to her shows, and her hard work and attention to detail made them worth watching. As a businesswoman she looked forward to building a career in television that was made to last. "I want to be a house, not a car," she said. "A hot red sports car is cool. But in a couple of years it starts looking a little rusty, so you get a new one. And that's the way it is with those hot careers."[77]

Rather than being a star who grabbed the spotlight and then faded quickly, Banks looked forward to establishing a career that gained in value. To do this, she took steps to continue to be a force in television and looked for relevant issues her audience could identify with. She had long been an advocate of inner beauty but knew how to attract an audience with glamour, good looks, and interesting topics. By producing television shows that contained both elements of beauty as well as a thoughtful side, she found her niche in the television industry.

Chapter 7

A Growing Empire

Banks had become a powerful woman with a message to deliver. She consistently emphasized the importance of the strength and beauty that come from inside a person, and delivered this message with a glamorous edge. She successfully made this point with her reality program and talk show, and her earning power and presence on television brought her to the attention of people in the world of business. Banks was included on the lists of the most influential celebrities in *Time* (in 2007) and *Forbes* (from 2005 to 2008) for her programs such as TZONE and her ability to create appealing television programs.

Banks wanted her shows to make a difference in the lives of the people who were on her programs as well as those of her viewers, so she explored socially relevant topics as well as delivered entertainment to her audience. She remained heavily involved with the details and production of her talk show to make sure it conveyed the message she wanted. She had long worked in an industry built on beauty, and now wanted to be a role model for something other than looks. "I want the shows to provide social commentary," she said. "The shows I'm producing aren't just hair and makeup and 'Oh, your heart is broken'—it's racism and inter-racial dating."[78]

Painful Criticism

Banks herself knew how difficult it was to live up to the image of a model's good looks. In early 2007 she went to Australia

Healthy Living

Banks wanted women to have a positive image about the way they looked and encouraged healthy eating and exercise habits. She said that loving yourself did not mean eating fast food all time—it meant eating healthy foods. It also meant staying fit with exercise.

True to form, she admitted she was not perfect when it came to working out. She sometimes went for months without exercising. Then she would get into an exercise routine that had her running three miles on a treadmill. "Hey," she says, "I'm only human. When I see someone running around without any cellulite, I think, Gosh, I wish my butt could be that smooth. But doing what I can to take care of myself means I don't worry about that so much."

Claire Connors, "Why I Love My Body…Just the Way It Is," *Shape,* June 2007, p. 63.

to film *America's Next Top Model.* As she showed the aspiring models how to model a swimsuit, photos were taken of her on the beach. The blurry and unflattering photos appeared to show that she was overweight. Tabloids published the pictures with headlines that proclaimed her "America's Next Top Waddle" and "Tyra Porkchop."[79]

There were reports she had gained forty pounds, and Banks received calls from family and friends who were worried about her health. Banks said she had not gained that much weight and had no concerns with her looks. At first she tried to laugh off the false reports and not care about them, but she could not help being concerned about what people were saying about her. She was hurt that people were being so mean about her appearance. "It was such a strange meanness and rejoicing that people had when thinking that was what my body looked like," she said. "It was really hurtful to me."[80]

Banks enjoyed her post-modeling curves and was deeply hurt when her weight was critiqued by the public.

Facing Her Critics

Banks came to realize that she could not let the criticism go by without responding to it. She was ready to tell her side of the story. "I could have ignored it, but instead chose to keep it real and addressed it right on the stage in front of my audience—while wearing the swimsuit," she said.[81]

On her show Banks showed people the truth about her body and was candid about her feelings about how she looked. She wore the swimsuit to show she was not ashamed of her body and teared up as she spoke about how the comments about her body had hurt her. She admitted to gaining thirty pounds since her days as a *Sports Illustrated* swimsuit model, but others noted that, at her height of five feet and ten inches, she was at a healthy weight of 161 pounds. Her weight did not bother her, she said, but comments from other people did. "I've made millions of dollars with the body I have, so where's the pain in that?" she said. "If I was in pain, I would have dieted. The pain is not there—the pain is someone printing a picture of me and saying those [horrible] things."[82]

"So What?"

Banks did not hide the fact that she had gained some weight since her modeling days, and her old jeans no longer fit the way they used to. She liked being at a slightly lighter weight, but admitted she did not have the discipline to do the workouts that weight loss required. She made it her goal to spread the word that women could be happy with their looks as they were. Aspiring to be model thin was not healthy, and Banks wanted women to realize that. She talked openly about her weight and appearance as well as the painful side of what people said about her.

Through her talk show, she began a "So What?" campaign, encouraging women to combat negative statements about their weight with that retort. She talked about it on her show, led a march of women wearing red tube tops in Los Angeles, and encouraged women to share their own "So What?" moments through a blog. "I was raised by women who don't believe that

Through her show Banks launched the "So What?" campaign for women to embrace their size as she had.

being super-skinny is the epitome of beauty," she said. "Being the best that you can be? That's beautiful, and I wanted to find a way to encourage every woman to love her body."[83]

Banks wanted those who admired her as a role model to realize that women often questioned whether their bodies looked right. She emphasized that she was happy with how she looked. "So many young girls are looking at that," Banks said. "I need to let them know that's not ugly."[84]

Banks turned the jabs at her weight into an opportunity to help people make their lives better. She had taken a chance by speaking out about her weight and revealing what her body looked like, and it paid off with a popular campaign that helped other women feel better about their bodies. She was enthusiastic about encouraging other women to take chances with their lives as well and to change things for the better. "I get a lot of feedback from my audience whenever I talk about how to take chances,"

Tyra's Tips for Feeling Better

Tyra Banks wanted women to have a positive image of their bodies and had some suggestions for women who wanted to feel better about themselves. Repeating affirming words goes a long way toward giving a woman confidence, she suggested. "Look in the mirror and find one thing that you love about yourself and say it aloud," she said. "The next day find another thing and accentuate that."

She also recommended that a woman have some time to herself to stay healthy. When Tyra feels stressed or overwhelmed, she goes to a spa for a massage and some quiet time. She also uses deep breathing to help her relax. "Everyone needs to breathe and take a break," she said.

Hallie Levine Sklar, "Women Who Shape the World," *Shape,* November 2007, p. 168.

she noted. "I'm a big believer in making a plan, and I want to empower this generation and help them feel they can get out there and make a difference in the world. It's about sharing what I did with my life and helping them do it in their lives."[85]

Little Time for Romance

Banks had a busy and successful career and was not afraid to face her critics. Her schedule left little time for dating, however, and Banks had difficulty finding a man who was not overwhelmed by her success. She did not want someone who was only interested in dating her because she was famous and a supermodel, and she needed someone who understood her hectic lifestyle. Her boyfriend would need to handle the fact that she was a well-known celebrity who was on television everyday.

She initially thought the talk show would make it easier for her to find a boyfriend who appreciated her for who she was, because the show allowed her true personality to emerge and took some of the shine off her supermodel label. Yet, she still had trouble finding a man who meshed with her personality. "I always tell a guy that I'm dating: I don't need you, I want you. But a lot of them are like"—alarmed face—"I want you to need me. I don't want you to want me!"[86]

Banks dated investment banker John Utendahl, and, when she moved the filming of her talk show from Los Angeles to New York, some thought it was to live closer to him. She insisted she did not make the move because of their relationship. "I would never move a show for a man," she said. "I prefer the pace and excitement of New York to Los Angeles. I feel so alive in New York—the city seems to fuel my brain."[87]

Continuing to Captivate

The California native moved from Los Angeles to New York City for her talk show's third season and strove to deliver programs that were relevant to viewers. "I want to be able to help as many women as possible realize their ambitions and dreams. I know

Banks and girls from cycle 10 of America's Next Top Model. *She never thought the show would be so successful to reach a 10th season.*

I'm helping people already, and that's very rewarding. But there's always more to do, and I won't rest until the show is even bigger and better," she said.[88]

Banks's *Top Model* show also remained a favorite with viewers. In 2007 the show's eighth cycle began, and critic Lisa Schwarzbaum was amazed by its enduring popularity. She admitted she was again drawn in by the show. "By now ANTM runs like a dream, a crazed circus of hair snarls and temperament snarls. Who's on top? The answer is easy: all of us slobs who get to judge at home," Schwarzbaum said.[89]

Although Banks did not spend as much time with the show as she had at when it began, she remained involved in the details of production, such as the opening photo of the show's contestants. Banks pulled back a bit from her appearances on the show to balance all that she was doing with her talk show, but when the tenth cycle of America's Next Top Model began in February 2008, reviewer Tom Gliatto said it had not lost any of its punch. "Launching its tenth season, Tyra Banks's Top Model does not disappoint. A winningly silly free-for-all of catfights, fashion and camp, it makes Project Runway look like an academic conference," Gliatto said.[90]

Banks admitted that when she started the program, she never thought her show would have continued success it had. "I thought it was going to last for two seasons," says Banks. "Around season 5, I said, 'Ken, how far can we go—8?' He goes, 'I'm thinking 10.' Now we're at 10 and not stopping."[91]

The show remained so popular with modeling hopefuls that hundreds waited outside a New York City hotel for a chance to audition for cycle thirteen in March 2009. Several were injured when a stampede occurred as women rushed out of the area after a car on the street overheated and began smoking. There was so much chaos that auditions had to be canceled.

Banks made sure the show went on after the audition snafu. She apologized in the media to the girls who had been waiting for their chance to get on the show and rescheduled a better organized audition a month later.

Although Banks did not attend the auditions, she remained the focal point of America's Next Top Model. On the premiere of season twelve, she called herself the goddess of fierce and dressed in a Greco-Roman costume. She also continued to add new twists to keep viewers interested. For cycle thirteen, she changed a rule that stated that models had to be at least five-foot-seven. For the fall 2009 season of the show, models had to be shorter, not taller, than five-foot-seven.

Power Broker

Just as her presence dominated her *Top Model* show, Banks was now seen as a force in the entertainment industry as well. She had a worldwide television presence and was CEO of Bankable Productions. In 2008 Banks became the top-earning woman on prime-time television in the United States, earning $23 million as *The Tyra Banks Show* and *America's Next Top Model* propelled her to that level. She brought in more than 3 million viewers to *America's Next Top Model* and more than 1 million to the *Tyra Show*. Banks won a Daytime Emmy in 2008 for her talk show, produced a series of DVDs based on the young adult *Clique* books, and signed a multimillion-dollar production deal for TV and film through Warner Bros. Entertainment. She also became involved in real estate development and sold retail products. She had risen above her supermodel image to become a powerful business-woman. "Known solely as a pretty face for much of her career, Banks has reinvented herself as a power player in the entertainment industry—and more importantly, as a brand," reported writer Tim Stack.[92]

Banks won the Outstanding Talk Show Emmy in 2008.

Banks did not stop there, but remained a force behind more television programming. In fall 2008 Banks launched the reality show *Stylista*, which featured eleven young women competing for an editorial job with *Elle* magazine. The contestants worked as assistants to the magazine's fashion news director and carried out editorial assignments in each episode. As with *Top Model* they were judged on how they did, and one person was fired each week. The winner got a job at the magazine as well as a Manhattan apartment and a clothing allowance.

The show followed a popular format as it put contestants through challenges that could land them a job at the magazine but was criticized for trying to mimic the popular Meryl Streep movie *The Devil Wears Prada*, which looked at the workings of *Vogue* magazine. *New York Magazine* said the show was painful to watch. "It highlights in a painfully obvious way how desperately *Elle* wants to be *Vogue*," Chris Rovzar said. "And it's uncomfortable."[93]

True Beauty

Stylista did not make a return for the 2009 season, but Banks turned her attention to other projects. She produced yet another program in winter 2009, when she joined forces with actor and reality-show producer Ashton Kutcher to create the program *True Beauty*. Banks was an executive producer of the reality program hosted by actress Vanessa Minnillo that had six women and four men living in a mansion and competing for the title of "Most Beautiful."

The contestants knew they were being judged on their inner and outer beauty, how they respected their elders and how well they did in photo shoots. A panel of celebrities, including supermodel Cheryl Tiegs, judged the contestants. Critic Robert Bianco said the show had potential. "That doesn't mean you won't have to sit through bragging and back-biting, but this time, the perpetrators might be punished," he noted.[94]

Although Banks was not active on the air in *Stylista* or *True Beauty*, she was part of the behind-the-scenes development.

Role Models

Many young women looked up to Banks, but she had women she admired as well. She thought highly of Oprah Winfrey, Martha Stewart, and Angelina Jolie, all for different reasons. "I love Martha Stewart's business model; she's so true to her brand," Banks said. "Oprah Winfrey for obvious reasons…and Angelina Jolie, more someone I respect because she doesn't just say it, she does it."

Annie Garcelon, "Tyra Banks," *Vplus,* July 31, 2007, p. A12.

Her name gave the shows credibility, and, although she was less visible than on her talk show or *Top Model*, she saw this as a natural progression of her career. "It's good to be respected as a producer," she said. "That's the real power to make change."[95]

Making a Difference

Banks delivered shows with the message that women had more to offer than beauty. Her looks had given her the opportunity to be part of the entertainment industry, but she was a supermodel with a conscience who used that fame to develop programs that stressed a woman's inner beauty. Banks had a way of getting her point across that was intriguing and captivating to her audience as she created entertaining shows with a glamorous side while maintaining her girlfriend-next-door image. Her ability to connect with her audience had made her a powerful force in the entertainment industry, but she was not content to stop there. "Oprah Winfrey is a mogul. Martha Stewart is a mogul. I'm probably a mogul in the making," she said. "I'm almost there."[96]

Always focused on taking the next step, Banks moved decidedly from supermodel to television personality to media mogul.

Forbes magazine listed her as one of the most influential women in media in 2009, noting that she brought in $30 million. It was not power for power's sake that she was after, however. She strove to create shows that made an impact and helped women improve their self-esteem. "I can't change society," she said. "But I can help women feel good about themselves."[97]

Chapter 1: Gangly Girl, Beautiful Model

1. Tyra Banks and Vanessa Thomas Bush, *Tyra's Beauty Inside and Out*. New York: Harper Collins Publishers, 1998, p. 171.
2. Tyra Banks, "Confessions of a Former Mean Girl," *Teen People*, October 2005, p. 52.
3. Banks, "Confessions of a Former Mean Girl," p. 52.
4. Banks, "Confessions of a Former Mean Girl," p. 52.
5. Celeste Fremon, "Not Just Another Pretty Face," *Good Housekeeping*, October 2005, p. 164.
6. Banks et al, "What Matters Most in My Work and My Life," *Newsweek*, October 20, 2008, p. 54.
7. Banks et al, "What Matters Most in My Work and My Life," p. 54.
8. Banks et al, "What Matters Most in My Work and My Life," p. 54.
9. Banks et al, "What Matters Most in My Work and My Life," p. 54.
10. Tom Gliatto and Bryan Alexander, "Tyrasaurus," *People*, April 11, 1994, p. 57.

Chapter 2: High Fashion Model

11. Tyra Banks and Vanessa Thomas Bush, *Tyra's Beauty Inside and Out*, p. 171.
12. "Banks," *Cosmopolitan*, October 2005, p. 66.
13. "Tyra Banks," *People*, May 9, 1994, p. 118
14. Deborah Gregory, "Tyra Company," p. 60.
15. Allison Samuels, "Tyra Banks," *Newsweek*, August 25, 2003, p. 10.
16. Deborah Gregory, "Tyra Company," p. 60.
17. Deborah Gregory, "Tyra Company," p. 60.
18. Allison Adato and Amy Elisa Keith, "Tyra Talks," *People*, February 5, 2007, p. 82.
19. Adato and Keith, "Tyra Talks," p. 82.

Chapter 3: Supermodel Success

20. Deborah Gregory, "Tyra Company," p. 60.
21. Aldore Collier, "John Singleton: Higher Learning in Hollywood," *Ebony*, April 1995, p. 122.
22. Deborah Gregory, "Tyra Company," p. 60.
23. Collier, "John Singleton: Higher Learning in Hollywood," p. 122.
24. Carol Schatz and Vicki Sheff-Cahan, "Higher Yearning," *People*, January 23, 1995, p. 83.
25. Schatz and Sheff-Cahan, "Higher Yearning," p. 83.
26. Deborah Gregory, "Tyra Company," p. 60.
27. "Movies," *Rolling Stone*, January 26, 1995, p. 66.
28. Richard Schickel, "By the Dots," *Time*, January 23, 1995, p. 57.
29. Janet Maslin, "Higher Learning: Short Course in Racism on a College Campus," *New York Times*, January 11, 1995, p. 13.
30. Jonathan Van Meter, "Tyra and Spoon," *Women's Sports & Fitness*, June 1998, p. 334.
31. Adato and Keith, "Tyra Talks," p. 82.
32. Lynn Norment, "Tyra Banks: On Top of the World," *Ebony*, May 1997, p. 110.
33. Banks et al, "What Matters Most in My Work and My Life," p. 54.
34. Tim Stack, "America's Next Top Mogul," *Entertainment Weekly*, February 22, 2008, p. 28.

Chapter 4: Role Model and Mentor

35. Nancy Jo Sales, "A Model Mogul," *Vanity Fair*, February 2007, p. 168.
36. Tyra Banks and Vanessa Thomas Bush, *Tyra's Beauty Inside and Out*, p. 171.
37. Renee Minus White, "Tyra Tips off Teens with New Beauty Book," *New York Amsterdam News*, April 9, 1998, p. 17.
38. John Griffiths, "Just One of the Girls," *Health*, November 2003, p. 120.
39. Griffiths, "Just One of the Girls," p. 120.

40. Griffiths, "Just One of the Girls," p. 120.
41. Adato and Keith, "Tyra Talks," p. 82.
42. Griffiths, "Just One of the Girls," p. 120.
43. Jeannie Kim, "Mothers and Shakers 2002," *Redbook*, October 2003, p. 118.
44. Banks, "Confessions of a Former Mean Girl," p. 52.
45. Maya Browne, "Tyra for Real," *Heart and Soul*, December 1996/January 1997, p. 28.
46. Lynn Hirschberg, "Banksable," *The New York Times*, June 1, 2008. www.nytimes.com/2008/06/01/magazine/01tyra-t.html?.

Chapter 5: Top Model

47. Marc Peyser and Allison Samuels, "Tyra Inc.," *Newsweek*, March 15, 2004, p. 58.
48. Stack, "America's Next Top Mogul," p. 28.
49. Peyser and Samuels, "Tyra Inc.," p. 58.
50. Ting Yu et al, "Pop Quiz with Tyra Banks," *People*, June 2, 2003, p. 24.
51. Chuck Barney, "UPN Banking on Tyra for 'Top Model,'" *Contra Costa Times*, January 16, 2003.
52. Bill Keveney, "Banks Cashes in on Clout from 'Top Model,'" *USA Today*, February 23, 2004, p. 03d.
53. Jennifer Armstrong, "Clothes Knit Group," *Entertainment Weekly*, January 16, 2004, p. 62.
54. Lee Alan Hill, "'Top Model' Delivers the Ratings, Demo UPN Wants," *Television Week*, January 31, 2005, p. 12.
55. Marc Peyser and Allison Samuels, "The Tyra Typhoon," *Newsweek*, March 22, 2004, p. 10.

Chapter 6: Talk Show Star

56. Celeste Fremon, "Not Just Another Pretty Face," *Good Housekeeping,* October 2005, p. 164.
57. Juan Morales, "Tyra Banks," *Redbook*, April 2006, p. 136.
58. Christopher Lisotta, "Tyra Banks," *Television Week*, January 10, 2005, p. 49.
59. Lisotta, "Tyra Banks," p. 49.

60. Christopher Lisotta, "*Model's* Banks Signs for Talker," *Television Week*, October 4, 2004, p. 14.

61. Andy Serwer, "From Top Model to Young Oprah," *Fortune*, February 20, 2006, p. 28.

62. "Tyra Banks Proves Her Breasts Are Real," Associated Press, http://www.msnbc.msn.com/id/9427670/.

63. Fremon, "Not Just Another Pretty Face," p. 164.

64. "The Tyra Banks Show vs. America's Next Top Model," *People*, November 28, 2005, p. 56.

65. Allison Waldman, "Personal Touch Makes Tyra Unique," *Television Week*, April 23, 2007, p. 24.

66. Greta Van Susteren, "Tyra Banks Goes Undercover," *On the Record with Greta Van Susteren* (FOX News), November 1, 2006.

67. Waldman, "Personal Touch Makes Tyra Unique," p. 24.

68. Waldman, "Personal Touch Makes Tyra Unique," p. 24.

69. Alisa Gumbs, "Model Inc.," *Black Enterprise*, September 2006, p. 112.

70. Nancy Jo Sales, "A Model Mogul," *Vanity Fair*, February 2007, p. 168.

71. Tim Stack, "Mad TV," *Entertainment Weekly*, April 29, 2005, p. 22.

72. Sales, "A Model Mogul," p. 168.

73. "The Tyra Banks Show vs. America's Next Top Model," p. 56.

74. Gumbs, "Model Inc.," p. 112.

75. Heidi Klum, "Supermogul with A Business Model," *Time*, May 8, 2006, p. 158.

76. Klum, "Supermogul with A Business Model," p. 158.

77. Morales, "Tyra Banks," p. 136.

Chapter 7: A Growing Empire

78. Sales, "A Model Mogul," p. 168.

79. Claire Connors, "Why I Love My Body…Just the Way It Is," *Shape*, June 2007, p. 63.

80. Adato and Keith, "Tyra Talks," p. 82.

81. Waldman, "Personal Touch Makes Tyra Unique," p. 24.

82. Adato and Keith, "Tyra Talks," p. 82.
83. Connors, "Why I Love My Body…Just the Way It Is," p. 63.
84. Rebecca Winters Keegan, "Not Fat, but Happy," *Time*, February 12, 2007, p. 99.
85. Waldman, "Personal Touch Makes Tyra Unique," p. 24.
86. Sales, "A Model Mogul," p. 168.
87. Lynn Hirschberg, "Banksable," www.nytimes.com/2008/06/01/magazine/01tyra-t.html?.
88. Waldman, "Personal Touch Makes Tyra Unique," p. 24.
89. Lisa Schwarzbaum, "Tube 'Tops,'" *Entertainment Weekly*, March 2, 2007, p. 59.
90. Tom Gliatto, "America's Next Top Model," *People*, February 25, 2008, p. 39.
91. Stack, "America's Next Top Mogul," p. 28.
92. Stack, "America's Next Top Mogul," p. 28.
93. Chris Rovzar, "Why We're Embarrassed for 'Elle,' Anne Slowey and 'Stylista,'" *New York Magazine*, http://nymag.com/daily/fashion/2008/05/why_we_are_embarrassed_for_ann.html.
94. Robert Bianco, "Critics Picks," *USA Today*, January 5, 2009, p. 06d.
95. Jeannine Amber, "Standing in the Spotlight," *Essence*, February 2008, p. 23.
96. Stack, "America's Next Top Mogul," p. 28.
97. Laurie Sandell, "Tyra Banks: The Media Mogul," *Glamour*, www.glamour.com/women-of-the-year/2008/tyra-banks

1973

Tyra Lynne Banks is born on December 4 in Inglewood, California, near Los Angeles.

1991

Tyra graduates from Immaculate Heart High School in Los Angeles. She heads to Paris to give modeling a try and lands twenty-five runway jobs for designers such as Yves Saint Laurent, Oscar de la Renta, and Chanel.

1993

Banks appears on several episodes of *The Fresh Prince of Bel-Air* as Will Smith's girlfriend Jackie Ames.

The supermodel signs a deal with Cover Girl and is in the *Sports Illustrated* swimsuit issue. She also graces the covers of *Essence* and *Elle*.

1995

The role of Deja in the movie *Higher Learning* is Banks's big-screen acting debut.

1996

Banks makes history as the first black model on the cover of *Sports Illustrated*. She appears in a leopard spotted bikini alongside Valeria Mazza.

She also appears on the cover of *GQ* and the Victoria's Secret catalog.

1997

Banks again graces the cover of *Sports Illustrated*, this time alone. Her acting career continues with small roles as she appears in the program *New York Undercover* as Natasha Claybourne.

1998

Banks co-authors the book *Tyra's Beauty Inside and Out* that presents fashion tips as well as information on inner beauty.

1999

Banks begins her TZONE Foundation, offering support for girls through camps and grants.

2000

Banks plays the character Eve, a doll who comes to life, in the television move *Life Size*, appears in several episodes of the television show *Felicity* as Jane Scott, and acts in the film *Coyote Ugly*.

2002

Banks plays Nora in the movie *Halloween: Resurrection*.

2003

America's Next Top Model debuts with Banks as its star and executive producer.

2005

The Tyra Banks Show, a daytime talk show starring Banks, premieres in September.

2006

Banks retires from modeling. *Time* magazine names her one of the most influential people in the world.

2007

Banks moves production of her talk show from Los Angeles to New York.

Her production company, Bankable Productions, signs a deal with Warner Brothers to create primetime television programming.

She founds Bankable Enterprises to give her the opportunity to expand into non-film business opportunities.

2008

Banks wins a daytime Emmy for *The Tyra Banks Show*. She is an executive producer of the television show *Stylista*.

She confronts reports that she's too heavy by wearing a swimsuit on her television show and on the cover of *People* magazine. She is named one of *People*'s "100 Most Beautiful."

Her TZONE Foundation awards $40,000 in grants to four non-profits that promote positive female role models and encourage sisterhood among girls and young women.

2009

Banks works with Ashton Kutcher as an executive producer on the program *True Beauty*.

Forbes magazine lists her as one of the most influential women in media.

Banks continues to host her talk show and prepares to launch the thirteenth cycle of *America's Next Top Model*.

Books

Tyra Banks and Vanessa Thomas Bush, *Tyra's Beauty Inside and Out*, New York: HarperPerennial, 1998. Banks offers tips to girls and young women on applying makeup and polishing personality.

Karen Schweitzer, *Tyra Banks*, Broomall, Pennsylvania: Mason Crest Publishers, 2008. This brief and colorful biography offers a conversational overview of the life of the supermodel and television show producer as well as a number of photos of the star.

Anne Hill, *Gateway Biographies: Tyra Banks*, Minneapolis, Minnesota: Learner Publishing Group, 2009. This book for grades four to eight presents a look at Banks's life.

Periodicals

Lynn Hirschberg, "Banksable," *The New York Times,* June 1, 2006. http://www.nytimes.com/2008/06/01/magazine/01tyra-t.html. The article offers a detailed look at what Tyra Banks goes through to produce her shows and offers insights into her background.

Laurie Sandell, "Tyra Banks," *Glamour*, December 2008, p. 222. The magazine names Banks as one of the most influential women of 2008 and looks at her accomplishments.

Web Sites

Tyra Banks (www.tyrabanks.com). The official site for Tyra Banks presents information on her background and current projects.

The Tyra Banks Show (http://tyrashow.warnerbros.com/). This Web site for Banks's talk show offers a look at the topics featured on coming episodes and also offers fans the opportunity to chat and have their questions answered.

America's Next Top Model (http://www.cwtv.com/shows/americas-next-top-model). This site for Banks's reality show featuring a modeling competition offers information on the contestants as well as photos and a trivia game.

TZONE Foundation (www.tzonefoundation.org). Information about Banks's foundation is available from this site.

Terri Dougherty enjoys writing biographies and other books, and is the author of more than 80 titles. She lives in Appleton, Wisconsin, with her husband and three children, Kyle, Rachel, and Emily. She is very thankful that her daughters introduced her to *America's Next Top Model*.